Gordon Ramsay's

Playing with Fire

HarperCollins*Publishers*

HarperCollins*Publishers*
77–85 Fulham Palace Road,
Hammersmith, London W6 8JB

The HarperCollins website address is: www.harpercollins.co.uk

First published by HarperCollins*Publishers* 2007
This paperback edition published 2008

1 3 5 7 9 10 8 6 4 2

© Gordon Ramsay 2007, 2008

Gordon Ramsay asserts the moral right to be
identified as the author of this work

A catalogue record of this book is
available from the British Library

ISBN-13 978-0-00-725988-5
ISBN-10 0-00-725988-3

Printed and bound in Great Britain by
Clays Ltd, St Ives plc

Picture acknowledgements: Jonathan Glynn-Smith: p1; Paul Raeside:
p2 (top and left), p3 (top), p4 (both), p10 (top); Gordon Ramsay
Holdings: p2 (right), p7 (top); Sam Bailey: p3 (bottom); Ben Anders:
p5; Richard Baker Furniture: p6 (top); David Joseph: p7 (bottom);
John Carey: p8; Glen Dearing: p9 (both), p14, p16; Richard
Young/Rex Features: p10 (bottom), p11 (top); Simply-Photography,
London: p11 (bottom); Peter Sandground: p12 (top); AFP/Getty
Images: p12 (bottom); Getty Images: p13; Nicky Johnson: p15

While every effort has been made to trace the owners of copyright
material reproduced herein, the publishers would like to apologise for
any omissions and will be pleased to incorporate missing
acknowledgements in any future correspondence.

Mixed Sources
Product group from well-managed
forests and other controlled sources
www.fsc.org Cert no. SW-COC-1806
© 1996 Forest Stewardship Council
FSC

Contents

THE BEGINNING

And in the beginning,
there was nothing.

NOT A SAUSAGE – penniless, broke, fucking nothing – and although, at a certain age, that didn't matter hugely, there came a time when hand-me-downs, cast-offs and football boots of odd sizes all pointed to a problem that seemed to have afflicted me, my mum, my sisters, Ronnie and the whole lot of us. It was as though we had been dealt the 'all-time dysfunctional' poker hand.

I wish I could say that, from this point on, the penny had dropped and I decided to do something about it, but it wasn't like that. It would take years before there was any significant change – before, as they say, I had a pot to piss in.

This is the story of how that change took place.

CHAPTER ONE

EARLY DAYS

Work and opportunity come hand in hand,
but don't miss the big picture.

MONEY ONLY CAME into my life when I received my first
weekly wage. It came in a brown envelope with my name
on it, and its contents disappeared faster than Jack Rabbit
looking down the barrels of a sawn-off shotgun. Whatever
money might have come in during my all-too-brief football
days, my dad 'handled' for me. Whether it paid for his
booze or his musical dreams, I don't know, but very little of
it came my way, and I'm pretty sure Mum didn't see much
of it either. To be honest, I was far too busy trying to be
good at football to worry about it much, but in later years
– much later years – I think it brought on an almost patho-
logical need to know where my earnings went, who was
handling them, and God help anyone who couldn't explain
what was happening.

This way of working, to climb the greasy pole of recognition rather than earn a living, followed me right through
the early kitchens, where the only aim in this war zone was
learning how to be the best. I think that this need to be the
best was something that was always with me. It was, in the

first instance, nothing more than a competitive streak. If I was racing my snail against the field, then mine would have to win. If I was washing pots, then mine were the cleanest, driest, and finished in the shortest time.

But after a while, this changed. I began to take notice of the competition around me and, in doing so, I realized that I was much keener to get on and do things in a way that blitzed everyone around me out of the water. Being the best was like a vanity, and I became ever-conscious that just being better was nowhere near enough. I had to attain a height that was unassailable by others.

To do this was to search out teachers, example-setters, heroes, whatever. Anybody that could point the way forward was someone whom I needed to know. The early chefs of my teenage years were not always easy to get near, but, in time, they picked up on me. They knew that there was one hungry little bastard in their kitchens and that I would do anything, work without stopping, and consume every scrap of guidance.

All I wanted was to understand how to do something, and I was the fastest learner they would ever meet. Those chefs who were good (and by that I mean lived in three dimensions) watched and encouraged me. Those with a single dimension carried on frying eggs.

As I continued along this culinary towpath, I began to see that, not only was it necessary to learn my trade thoroughly, but to try and move it up a gear. What I also noticed was that, while it was relatively easy for me to do this, nobody else seemed so driven. For me, it was just natural, the only route, and I used to listen to my mates argue and complain about conditions, the hours, the pay. All these things I couldn't give a flying fuck about, to be honest.

Was I ever jealous of anyone who seemed to be ahead of me? No, that was never going to happen. That person became just a milestone and someone I would overtake as fast as possible. It was just like being a car in a race, and all the other cars were there to be overtaken. Even now, that is very much the case. The only difference is that it's no longer about being the best pot washer. Now I look for more Michelin stars than anyone else, I need to have the highest audience ratings on my TV shows, and I need to sell more books than all the other celebrity chefs.

Am I always successful at being the best? Am I fuck. Instead, I just think of Jack Nicholson in *One Flew Over the Cuckoo's Nest* when he tells his fellow inmates that he can tear the faucet from the floor and throw it through the window. They take bets because this boast just isn't going to happen. The camera watches him struggle, sweat and grunt until it is clear that the faucet is staying where it is. Nicholson eventually stops and looks around. 'Well, at least I tried, which is more than you bastards did,' he says. That's me. Just sometimes I aim too high and fail, but it will never stop me shooting for the stars. I might quietly have to accept that Jamie is going to sell more books than I am. For now.

In the meantime, the hours were forever and blotted out any time in which to think about money, far less spend it.

Time off was also for sleeping. Seventeen-hour shifts, an hour each way for travel, and the rest was for sleep. A day off once a week was also for sleeping. All fucking day. I needed rent money and I needed cash for fares, and then it was all gone. No movies, no restaurants, no cars, and I never drank.

After kitchens in London, my days in Paris were no different. I had gone there, as I knew that that was still the home of fine dining, and I was searching for the places that would inspire and teach me. This was my choice, even if at the beginning I couldn't speak any French and knew no one. There was a constant obsession with learning, with looking for respect in a kitchen where the culture was to be as dismissive as a fly swatter. Asking for a rise was as far from my mind as ringing in with a sickie.

In time, I returned to London and started working with Pierre Koffmann at *La Tante Claire*. It was while I was there that I was approached by a diminutive Italian with an offer to start a new restaurant down some back street off the Fulham Road. When you have nothing except your knives, when everyone insists that you are nothing but a piece of shit on their shoes, a kind word with the promise of recognition and money is like discovering a high pair in your dysfunctional poker hand. Suddenly, there was someone inviting me to run their kitchen for them. I was going to be called 'Chef', with my own small brigade and, moreover, there might be some proper money on the table. The restaurant was to be called *Aubergine*.

A pair in cards seems a lot when you have nothing. It blots out the fact that all the other players might have a better hand, and the last thing on their minds around the table is your welfare. But, suddenly, here was this god-forsaken, beaten-up old restaurant site that had already had a long history of failure. Had I but known it, this was the last-chance saloon for the Italian owners who had somehow gotten it into their minds that I could save the day for them.

Too bloody right. The salary was better than I could ever have imagined, and all I had to do was what I do best.

I had come back from Paris in 1993 and started *Aubergine* not long afterwards, by which time I was twenty-seven and the owner of a flat. Well, not quite a whole flat, as I went halves with a mate and we and the Building Society were the proud owners together. We let one room out, but were either too busy or too exhausted to collect the rent. The tenant didn't come up with the goods very often, so one way or another, it was always a fucking fight to pay the mortgage.

From this early desperation, I suddenly had a boat to steer in the form of *Aubergine*, and it would not be long before I was getting married. Another thing happened that would also have one fucking big effect on my life, and that was meeting the father of my wife, Tana.

I had met Chris earlier on when Tana was dating another chef who, anticipating wedding bells, had brought her and her parents to *Aubergine* on the second night that I was open. I had gone up to their table, sat down and told them about how things were going. A nice, informal little chat and then they were gone. I learned later that Chris, Tana's dad, had said to his wife, Greta, that I was totally preoccupied with myself and right up my own arse. Greta apparently smiled sweetly and said that I reminded her of Chris at that age. It wouldn't be long before Chris would be playing a central role in this story.

Either way, Tana fell out with this other dickhead of a chef and, before I knew it, we were dating and got married in December 1996. In the meantime, *Aubergine* was fast becoming a big hit and I was earning £6,000 a month. £6,000 a month! My mate, the Building Society and I sold the flat, and Tana and I were able to put down a deposit on part of an old school building in Battersea. We moved in, and suddenly there was a seismic shift in my life because *Aubergine* had become a phenomenon.

The *Aubergine* phenomenon is interesting. This was the stage, this tiny little fledgling restaurant, where I started to make a name for myself, where I was suddenly the unknown winger who was filling the goal net every Saturday to the extent that the press looked up and started mapping out my future as a name in their columns. Newspapers, magazines and the restaurant media are always looking for the next story, and they hooked on to me big time. Why did this previously unknown, off-street restaurant suddenly have the most sought-after reservations book in London?

Celebrity status didn't exist. Gordon Ramsay was a name that rolled off the tongue like broken glass, and the place had started on a shoestring with no big design budget, no PR and no launch party with 200 C-list celebs. If the truth were known, I didn't really know what PR stood for. What worked was that I was putting superbly executed, modern European dishes on the menu at the lowest prices. When I look at an old *Aubergine* menu now, we were selling – no, giving away – three courses for £18. I also had the makings of a strong, motivated staff in both the kitchen and the dining room. The staff were all young and all looking for classical training. The hardship that we were enduring in the kitchen was probably the glue that bonded us all together. They could see me pitching in, and maybe stories of my days in Paris, mixed with the obvious dedication of working like a hungry dog, bonded us together. What would seal this bond was the success that suddenly swept over us. I had proved, with the help of my staff, that hard work and self-conviction really will work. What we all knew about was obsession and the pursuit of perfection, so every guest who came into the restaurant liked what they saw and went off to spread the word. It appealed to affluent locals who boasted about the little restaurant that they had discovered as though it were their own. No wonder I didn't need a poncy PR firm.

On the other hand, it was also a question of timing. I can't take any credit for that. We just happened to be pursuing perfection at exactly the right time and place.

And there also were at least two vital things I didn't yet understand.

One was that those days were producing what would be a fantastic stable of chefs-in-waiting who, one day, would put Gordon Ramsay on the world stage. I didn't know that's what I was doing when I hired them or when we worked alongside each other to get it right every time. I didn't know it then, but they would be one of the most important factors in my later success.

The other issue was that, as successful as *Aubergine* was, I was doing everything wrong if I wanted to make money and run a business. The restaurant was certainly making money, but it wasn't my money, and my head was buried in a hot stove all day. I had no understanding of the horizon, no wider picture, and – at least then – I didn't realize how much I had become a means for others to feather their own nests.

The situation would not last.

CHAPTER TWO

FIRST STEP ON THE LADDER

Before diving in, break the ice and
think through the basics.

AUBERGINE WAS OWNED by people who were more interested in the money than the food, and this was the lesser
known side of the story. The constant rowing and the politics that spilled over from the boardroom were soon having
an effect on me, and as the restaurant grew more successful, plans were being hatched for laying a string of golden
eggs. And they would be spilling out of my arse. Pizza
parlours and roll-outs featured regularly in the boardroom
plans, and I knew that it was time to go.

I had been given 10 per cent of the shares in the firm that
owned *Aubergine* and, occasionally, a few thousand pounds
came my way as a sort of drip-feed to keep me happy. But
with each director trying to secure my support against their
opposing number, I soon began to look around in spite of
the stratospheric reputation of *Aubergine*. My problem was
that I just hadn't thought through what I was really after.
That was the first lesson I needed to learn.

From out of the blue, a small hotel operator called David Levin approached me to take charge of his restaurant, which had just lost its Michelin-starred chef. Before I knew it, he had offered me £150,000 a year and 5 per cent of the profits. Fuck me. This was double what I was earning, and I could see that the site in Mayfair was just right for the three Michelin stars. They shone in my mind much brighter than any share certificates or, come to think of it, any roll-out Italian pizza parlours.

However, although I had had lots of talks with David, I was a bit confused about how this might all pan out. There was a son who was clearly going to take over the business at some time, and in the back of my mind, I was wondering why the other chef had left. I can't say that it was a case of once bitten, but I had acquired a sixth sense about who really might be my friend and who might ultimately sell me down the river in a leaky sieve.

So I spoke to the one person who would have my interests at heart, and that was Chris, my father-in-law. I explained the offer and asked if he would meet with David and let me know what he thought. I didn't know it then, and I am fucking positive that Chris didn't give it a further thought, but this was the very first step we took together in the world of commerce. It was to be the initial, tentative coming together of two people who were totally different in their skills and ages. As time went on, these differences were to meld together in an unusual alliance, and it became clear that we were as alike as two wings on a plane.

The two old-timers met for lunch at *The Capital* and, like so many successful businessmen, David failed to listen to a thing Chris said about my ambitions or dreams. As far as he was concerned, it was a done deal and Chris was in the way. Be courteous enough to the father-in-law and he will, no doubt, go along with the grand plan.

I think that Chris was a little wary of trying to muscle in on my life and into a business that he knew very little about. Either way, it was not long before I was invited to the offices of Withers for what I thought was just another meeting. Chris agreed to come along, and there we were in front of three lawyers, none of whom was mine, and David's son. Apparently, David was on the golf course, treating today's procedures as a done deal. Chris looked puzzled as he scanned the documentation in front of him. One of the three lawyers smiled and indicated that this was a contract now awaiting my signature.

The kick under the table from Chris came as a surprise and fucking well hurt. It was to become a regular method of communication in later meetings when things were going wrong. Chris asked if we could have five minutes, and out of the room we went. He looked at me and asked two simple, amazing questions. 'Gordon, what do you really want to do in life? Do you want to work for someone, or do you want to go it alone?' I was beginning to realize, at last, that the world was beginning to rotate.

Ten minutes later, we had proffered our apologies to the signing committee, who, no doubt, relayed news of our departure to the golf course, and we were on our way out of this firm of very expensive lawyers.

We had, in that one moment, agreed to go it alone. Two unlikely partners and only a dream between us, and I had just learned an important lesson: you need to know what you're aiming for in order to reach it.

The saga at *Aubergine* still had another torturous six months to run. I was still refusing to sign any contract, especially as one of the clauses would bar me from opening a restaurant within a twenty-five-mile radius of *Aubergine* if I ever left. Franco Zanellato and Claudio Pulze sold their shares to Giuliano Lotto, giving him 90 per cent of the company, which meant he could do what he liked. What he liked, at this point, was to raise prices, move my staff around, and talk about strange plans for bistros in Bermuda. Of the three Italians, Giuliano, a former stockbroker, knew the least about the restaurant trade.

What we were now looking for was the big chance, and that chance suddenly appeared with a call from my old boss.

CHAPTER THREE

ROYAL HOSPITAL ROAD

When the time is right with plans,
designs, borrowings and staff,
mix them in a bowl with a
spoonful of intense passion.

IT IS STRANGE, but of all the influential chefs who have been documented in my life, the one who gave me the greatest leg-up is hardly ever mentioned. I had worked for Pierre Koffmann at *La Tante Claire*, and had even taken Marcus Wareing from him to be my right-hand man at *Aubergine*, and it was he who was about to give me the very opportunity that I needed.

Pierre had been running *La Tante Claire* for twelve years in a strange backwater of Chelsea called Royal Hospital Road. The road was named after the home of the Chelsea Pensioners, the retired ex-soldiers who bring colour to the area with their scarlet coats and incredible personal histories. It runs parallel to the River Thames from Pimlico to Cheyne Walk, a rat run where National Express buses come barrelling along to avoid the snarl-ups of the Embankment traffic, and its buildings camouflage a wealthy population of socialites and Sloanes.

I had worked at *La Tante Claire* as head chef after returning from France. It was a brief period of employment, marked by Pierre's disappearance the day before I arrived, leaving an enigmatic, dismissive note. He was on holiday, and a three-day handover before he entrusted me with his beautiful cuisine would have been helpful. But he was a man of few words and, being very French, had little time for anything except cooking and rugby.

La Tante Claire had three Michelin stars and, as such, it was a destination restaurant. It wouldn't have mattered where it was located because people sought it out as a centre of gastronomy. Any other restaurant in this location might have struggled if it relied on customers just passing by, as nobody ever did, except to buy a newspaper or walk the dog. But Pierre was comfortable there. He had a fabulous reputation and was happy to close seven weeks each year for holidays, as the French tend to do, and his staff were more than happy to follow suit.

I didn't really know why he wanted to move, but he had lost his wife not long before, and had also been offered the chance to move *La Tante Claire* to The Berkeley, a hotel that was part of the Savoy Group. So his immediate problem was how to shift the existing lease on the Royal Hospital Road restaurant, at which point his Gallic gaze fell on me. Would I be interested in buying the unexpired lease for £500,000? I had no money and, quite frankly, he could have been asking for £5 million. But this was where Chris came in. I was happy to sit on the sidelines and watch him deal with this tiny obstacle.

I had no idea about Chris's personal finances. What I did realize was that the money Pierre wanted would be just the half of it. There would be a much bigger bill if we were ever going to change this rather tired restaurant into Gordon Ramsay's début as a chef patron. That sort of money was just not lying around in people's bank accounts, and we were going to have to get involved in the world of banking.

Chris put together a proposal and sent it down the wire to a bank manager he had known and dealt with for years at the Bank of Scotland. Iain Stewart had been involved in earlier restaurant businesses at the highest culinary level, including none other than my much-respected boss in an earlier era, Albert Roux. This was lucky because it gave the bank an insight into the economics of Michelin-starred dining – what it cost, but also what it could earn. Claudio Pulze, one member of the Italian trio at *Aubergine*, once told Chris that a three-star restaurant could never make money. Fortunately for us, Iain Stewart had seen the living proof that Claudio was wrong, and he was able to reassure the bank's credit committee. This removed any lingering doubts that the bank might have had about lending us the money.

So I dug out my one and only suit from a very sparse wardrobe and set off with Chris to the old P&O building at the bottom of Trafalgar Square for an introductory meeting. I could feel my bollocks shrinking as I was shown into the meeting room with three or four banking individuals dressed in grey suits, blue-striped shirts and forgettable ties.

So forgettable, in fact, that I can remember little else. All the talking from our side came from Chris, and I just prayed that no incoming missile of a question came my way. Do you know today's price of a barrel of oil, Mr Ramsay? What return on your equity capital do you expect in Years Two and Three, Mr Ramsay? Fuck me. I kept my head between my shaking legs.

Just as I felt we were getting these people on our side, Chris suddenly let loose a tirade of abuse about greedy bankers who screwed their clients wherever they could. They had just suggested an administrative fee of a couple of thousand pounds, and Chris countered it with £500. I didn't know where the fuck to look. If this was business, then I would stay in the kitchen, where I could safely bollock my brigade without getting involved in any confrontation.

It was such a nightmare that I nearly missed the men in grey agreeing to Chris's revised figure. Their suggested £1,500 fee was big wonga, and not only had Chris saved it, but he had also shown me that bankers really can be wankers. The exception was Iain, who, I could see, had a sardonic smile on his face for much of this 'delicate' nego-tiating. He knew that what we were setting out to do was just the beginning of bigger stuff to come, and he was instrumental in these first, tentative steps.

Suddenly, the meeting was at an end, and there was this short-arsed, gritty Scot with a sharp eye and tongue smiling, shaking hands and wishing us well. Fuck. Easy as that.

But, of course, it wasn't quite so. It's one thing to borrow the money, but then you have to pay it back – with interest. Also, just as we were getting the loan agreed, there were things happening that would later have a big effect on my business. But at the time I didn't know that, and it just seemed to be threatening my deal. In fact, there seemed no solution. What had happened was that the Savoy Group had been approached by what was then an almost unknown financial animal called 'private equity'.

Private equity has become controversial for a number of reasons, and it is a familiar phrase today. It means powerful investment funds not available to the general public or traded on stock exchanges, which buy up companies in return for a share in the ownership. In this case, Blackstone Private Equity were the Savoy Group's suitors, and it was the first time that I ever heard the name that would become so important to us. On this occasion, they were offering over half a billion pounds to shareholders of the Savoy Group to buy Claridge's, The Connaught, The Berkeley and, of course, The Savoy.

Once this deal had gone through, the idea was that these private equity players would bring about changes to increase the value of the Savoy Group in order to make it saleable at a profit acceptable to their investors. The trouble was that it meant that everything to do with the Savoy Group was on hold while the deal was going on, and that included Pierre Koffmann's move, too – which, in turn, meant ours. Before we knew it, we were back on the streets looking for alternative premises. We searched and looked at half a dozen sites, and each new potential restaurant we saw made us realize that Royal Hospital Road was, by far, what we wanted most. It was heart breaking to accept that it just wasn't going to happen.

Months went by. Updates on the Blackstone front were hard to come by. Their deal had eventually gone through, and they were now busy thinking about a million different changes they wanted to make in the way the Savoy Group was run. Whether they wanted Pierre Koffmann or not was just one of the decisions that they would make in the fullness of time, and we just had to wait. Pierre's advisors had long ago stopped returning calls, and I could feel the deal going cold.

One of these advisors was a particularly irritating 'fixer', a slobby suit who had clearly eaten well and frequently at *La Tante Claire*. Perhaps he sensed that this cosy arrangement was coming to an end and, as it became clear that Pierre's deal with The Berkeley actually might happen after all, Slobby became more elusive. Luckily for us, there was a lively partner from Pierre's accountancy firm who grabbed the ball and ran with it. Without him, I think we would still be on the touchline.

The deal progressed, and suddenly, there we were in the offices of the lawyers who were acting for *La Tante Claire* with a mile-long paper trail of agreements, leases, indemnities and guarantees ready for Chris and me to sign. As the snowstorm came to a finish, the lawyers wheeled in lunch and champagne to mark this momentous occasion. In all the completion meetings that took place later – and there were a lot of them – this was the one I'll always remember. Not just because it was the first, but because of this small gesture of kinship and kindness.

The bank had sent down a lesser minion to make sure the right signatures were attached to the borrowings documents. He was last to leave, having drunk enough bubbly to match what he considered an onerous task.

It was, without doubt, a fucking relief. I could now be open about my plans. I could leave *Aubergine* and stop stalling about signing the contract they had been pressing on me. I could now tell Marco Pierre White that I would not be part of his stupid plans for the *Café Royal*, as I now had the beginnings of what I had dreamed about: my own restaurant.

But I owe Pierre Koffmann for more than just placing the opportunity of my own restaurant in front of me. I don't know whether or not he thought £500,000 would be more than I could afford, or whether or not he just wanted me to succeed, but, without me asking, he delayed payment of £175,000 for a year to let me get some cash flow coming through.

Even so, we now had this vast loan, with monthly interest payments to go with it. So you didn't have to be a partner in super-league finance like Blackstone to realize that, having bought this tiny little restaurant, we urgently needed to get it open. We now had a staff ready and waiting, because forty-six of them walked out of *Aubergine* when Giuliano Lotto sacked Marcus Wareing. We certainly had our menus set out, but we needed to make the restaurant look right – and there wasn't much time.

We decided to get help from a small interior design firm that I had come across on an earlier project. The problem was that, years earlier, Pierre Koffmann had commissioned David Collins, who was then unknown, to design his restaurant, and his design had become so much a part of *La Tante Claire* and its cuisine that, inevitably, everything had to come out. This left a concrete shell and just thirty days to build something in its place.

The concrete shell is always going to haunt me. No one really knows what makes a restaurant successful. There are only a few real variables: the food, the location, the design, the price, the staff, the ambience and the clientele. But every time you think it can't be too difficult to crack the code, up pops a restaurant that should fail because the food is overpriced and atrocious, the location is in the middle of a railway arch, the staff are arrogant arseholes or the clientele is fickle – and they have to eat in a concrete shell. We all know of examples. The amazing and galling thing is that sometimes they don't fail.

So here we were, spending enough money on a designer to pay the gross national product of some African country while we knew of a famous fish restaurant on 55th Street in New York that is full every lunch and dinner in its original concrete shell. But then, I also know of a restaurant where the food is not fit for a dog, the fit-out cost 5 million quid and the tables are booked like Wembley for the Cup Final.

So, on balance, we had to do something about the walls at *Royal Hospital Road*. We needed to extract some kind of ambience out of this concrete, and I hadn't a clue how to do that. The interior design firm came up with their ideas, simple and uninspiring, but easy to fabricate and install. Their one creative touch was to introduce us to an artist called Barnaby Gorton, who painted a large, dreamy figurescape in blue and grey for a bargain £10,000. His vision, speed and enthusiasm meant that we hung on to him for the future. It was a pattern that we followed with a range of people we were to meet later, and who became part of our team for years to come.

Even so, the timetable was fucking tight, and half an hour before we opened for our first evening service, the front desk was still being put together, the carpet was being vacuumed and the glasses polished. The night before, it suddenly occurred to me that the dining room was desperately bleak. There was empty shelving in recesses, and I remember coming up with some appropriate language for the fuckpots who had moved on from their design mission and forgotten the last chapter of their brief.

I called Chris, and he immediately took from his flat a collection of Murano glass. Just for the opening week, of course, until we could find something else, except that it stayed there for five years and became an iconic part of *Royal Hospital Road*.

In many ways, the building was the easiest part. We just had to get the builders to perform, and they did so with all the usual sucking of teeth, streams of tea and stonewalling of any question that required the answer: 'Yes, we will finish on time.' The transferring of staff from their *Aubergine* existence to *Royal Hospital Road* had been a sensitive part of this journey. When the crunch came and everyone walked away from *Aubergine* after the Marcus Wareing fiasco, the only meeting place we had was Chris's flat in Mayfair.

There we all sat around this vast oak table looking with ashen faces at Chris, who was about to announce the new dawn. I often think back to that evening. Chris was sitting there in front of them, having just agreed to move forward with this unlikely band of refugees from *Aubergine*, all looking imploringly at him. They needed to know that, shortly, they would be transferring to Chelsea in peace and without the Italians. I don't know what he was thinking, but it must have been nerve-racking for him, too. One of the partners in our firm of lawyers, Joelson Wilson & Co., who had known Chris for twenty years, asked him if he was sure he knew what he was doing. Nothing like a positive, well-timed question to boost morale.

The first few nights were soft openings to welcome family, friends and staff. These were dress rehearsals to give everyone confidence in what they were doing and to find the rhythm and flow between kitchen and dining room that you need in a well-run restaurant. By the time the first till-ringing night was upon us, we were ready. It was an exciting moment, and it was then – at about 8 p.m. – that the air conditioning suddenly went down in the kitchen and the temperature rose to a sweltering forty-five degrees. There was nothing to do but get on with it and wait for the engineers in the morning.

By midnight, sweaty from the kitchen, we were able to count our first day's takings. By the end of the first month, September 1998, we had made money. Of course, that didn't even come near to writing off the capital expenditure, but we knew we had a business that was making a trading profit, and this was a fucking great relief so early on. Within six months, we were clearing £50,000 every month, and our debt to the bank was beginning to come down. It meant we were able to draw the £175,000 from cash flow to pay the final tranche to Pierre Koffmann and thank him for his patience. The other indicator of success was that our reservations book was stuffed solid. I had restricted the bookings to one month ahead. I had learned from my *Aubergine* days that a reservations book without any time limit gave people the impression that they would never get a table, so they often simply gave up.

The whole concept of reservations is always tricky. You need a definite policy so that guests know the score. All sorts of myths have grown up around the reservations books of popular restaurants. Try calling *The Ivy* for a table at eight o'clock tomorrow evening, and all they will want to know is who you are. No fame is no name, and your chances of a table between the hours of six o'clock and 10.30 p.m. are slim. It became a joke at *Aubergine* that reservations could be bought or sold on a commodity market so that punters had to pay money to someone else – I never saw it – just to book a table, which ought to be free. No different to touts outside Twickenham, Wimbledon or Wembley.

Just as *The Ivy* sees celebrity table allocations as a commercial way to make the restaurant work, we had to have a plan, too. And it needed to be flexible. Think of table arrangements on two of the year's big restaurant dates, St Valentine's Day and Mothering Sunday. Who wants a table for four on St Valentine's Day? The reservations manager has to plan ahead to get as many twos in as possible. Mothering Sunday is a family day, and suddenly, we need tables of four and upwards. Outside these special days, there has to be a balance of twos, fours and more. Too many twos need a lot of space, more laundry, more staff, and usually less money is spent on drink – and that's a problem. Tables of four usually mean higher drinks bills. More guests bring a bonhomie, which means more wine being poured.

And whatever happened to the table for one? That's always there in my restaurants. It's never going to be a money-spinner, but any restaurant that refuses a single guest for a booking shouldn't be in the business. Few people eat on their own in a restaurant, but there are some blessed people who come just to taste the food. What greater compliment can there be? One of Chris's old haunts is a wonderful, laid-back restaurant called *Rules*, serving some great British dishes – coincidentally, it's London's oldest eating establishment – and there is a table that only accommodates one guest. I have never seen that table empty.

There are only forty-five seats at *Royal Hospital Road*, which makes things easier. When the bookings for a day are complete, that's it. If the Queen called after that and asked for a table for two that evening for herself and Philip, you'd have to offer up your apologies. There is no room to manoeuvre, short of calling a guest and cancelling their booking, and that, believe me, is never going to happen. In a bigger restaurant like *Gordon Ramsay at Claridge's*, it is easier to rearrange the bookings, and there, to be honest, we always have a table up our sleeve.

But when you're planning reservations, you have to time them. Imagine two fully booked restaurants, one where everybody turns up at the same time, and the other, where all tables arrive at fifteen-minute intervals. Which restaurant is going to perform better? You have to give the kitchen a chance, and our guests have learned to appreciate this. Not only are they happy to book for 8.15 p.m., rather than eight o'clock, but they actually turn up on time.

When I think back to the early days at *The Connaught*, the procession of the old school diners into the restaurant at eight o'clock was a living nightmare for Angela Hartnett, the head chef. Then there's the appearance of London's power brokers for lunch at *The Savoy Grill*, all on the dot of one o'clock. Of course, it's difficult for the kitchen to handle. Actually, it's a fucking nightmare.

People say that restaurants where you have to book can never attract people who are just passing by. It's nonsense. My favourite scenario is when a party of six or eight knocks on the door at *Royal Hospital Road* late on a Friday night and asks if there is a chance of a table. Too bloody right there is. You wheel them in and come to an understanding that they are more than welcome, provided we can serve them with whatever we have left. It means that we can empty the fridges for the weekend and have a large bill to round off the evening. And we make the guests happy, too.

That combination of good planning and passionate staff is exactly what you need to make a restaurant successful. It's all part of the mix that makes a brilliant restaurant stand out from an ordinary one. That was what we had set out to achieve, and it soon became clear that we were getting there. And, suddenly, there was the chance of doing it twice.

It was in this same period that we were offered a second restaurant right in the middle of St James's. Someone had thought they would run a restaurant for fun, bring their mates, and wondered why it had all gone pear-shaped. I had a look at it, with its trolley of sweating cheeses, white-painted piano and filthy kitchen. The menu was a disgrace, and the owner was flat broke.

Before the ink was dry on a hastily cobbled contract, the bailiffs moved in. But they were just a day too late. The builders were stripping the last remains of 33 St James's and we had secured our second premises. The name was to become *Pétrus*, and the chef I brought in was Marcus Wareing. He was the first person to experience the elevation from chef to a shareholding chef patron.

This was where the stable of chefs-in-waiting that I built up at *Aubergine* became a reality. We have been able to expand because we have brilliant chefs, and giving them a share in the ownership of new restaurants was to become the way forward for us. I knew that the chef would always be the most important player, and it became a rule that we never planned a restaurant without the chef. The location, the design and the front-of-house staff were all important, but first we had to work out who would be in charge of the kitchen.

Pétrus was not an easy site. The kitchen was below the dining room, and everything had to be carried upstairs. It was a long room without a central arrangement for guests, so familiar at *Royal Hospital Road*, and without the easy, comfortable ambience. But all of this was more than balanced because we had a passion and energy to get this restaurant up and running profitably, which is exactly what we did.

The next job was to find a name. The name *Pétrus* represented the very finest claret. I wrote to the owners, asking if I could use the name, and they agreed. It meant a considerable investment in the cellar: as well as all the usual bins, we decided we needed to carry one of the finest collections of this Bordeaux wine, all the way back to 1945. It made me think that what we were becoming was a purveyor of wine, rather than food. After all, you can't charge any more than £100 per head for the menu, but there is little or no limit on what people can spend on wine.

This is a kind of kick in the bollocks for someone like me, for whom the cuisine is all important. But the business reality – whether I liked it or not – is that wine provides us with the profit we need to keep going. And I was determined to keep going. It was less than one year since I had opened *Royal Hospital Road*, and already I had the beginnings of a stable of restaurants, and I simply had to make them both successful.

And, on occasion, I could live with wine taking priority over the menu. One night while I was in the kitchen at *Royal Hospital Road* and Chris was in the office in Fulham Road, we got a call from Marcus to say that a table of six bankers had ordered £13,000 from the wine list. The feeling was electric, and the voltage increased in line with the spend. When the bill increased to £27,000, Chris started to make old man noises about credit card clearance. By the time it had reached £44,000, we made the decision to remove all food charges from the bill. After all, what was £600 in the face of this extraordinary wine spend? By noon on the following day, the news had somehow leaked, with front-page coverage in *The Sydney Morning Herald* and *The Straits Times*. It was one of the few occasions when *Pétrus* was on everyone's lips.

CHAPTER FOUR

A SCOTTISH FAILURE

Vanity should carry a health warning.
When it bites you, take action.
Bleeding to death can kill you.

ROYAL HOSPITAL ROAD was paying its way. *Pétrus* was winning praise for Marcus Wareing's cuisine. We were confident and on the look out for more sites, but – as it turned out – I was sleepwalking into my first failure. Good lessons are best learned early, but they are never easy, as I was about to find out in an ice-cold, down-your-neck way from a wild foray into Scotland at a time when I was still learning to walk in a business nappy.

This is a story of vanity, plain and simple. Open a couple of successful restaurants in London, and you are ready to take on the world without it ever occurring to you that there might be factors you've never thought about before.

As is so often the case, it began with a phone call and a proposition at the end of the line. In this case, it was Edinburgh beckoning with a prime site on the Royal Mile, and Chris was off like a gunshot. First, he checked out the proposal, talked to the finance director, who was on show-round duty, and then moved off. He was up there for the rest of the day to have a look around the Edinburgh restaurant scene before getting an early flight back to London the next morning.

The idea was to see if we could offer something to the stiff, up-your-arse society of professionals, financiers and low-spending tourists who exist side by side in the city. We knew that the Scottish Parliament would soon be opening – if someone could just control the shocking building overspends of public money and long delays – and that would mean a fucking big boost to the local restaurant trade.

But when Chris got back, he was not optimistic. He told me how the beautiful Princes Street was now a ruin, and asked what the fuck had happened there. It's true: it's like there's been a hideous signage competition, with the world's worst performers strung out in a line, and nobody seems to notice it. It's plain fucking wicked that this has been allowed to happen. Is this the price of commerce? Business doesn't mean instant shit in the face like this. Whoever was in charge must have been blind or an idiot. What a sad, fucking shame.

Chris looked at a hundred different menus, checked the pricing and talked to bored waiting staff. A picture began to emerge, and he already knew that Edinburgh was not for us. Edinburgh makes money and keeps it. They spend it carefully and primly on school fees at Fettes or antique fireguards. There is no joy here, nothing that drives people out to get rat-arsed on a Friday in an Armani suit with a midnight call to the wife to hand supper to the dog.

There was a lovely story while Chris was up there. That evening, he got a cab over to Leith to try out Martin Wishart, who was making a name for himself in his restaurant by the quayside. As always, Chris was dressed in a suit, and having sat down, he went through the card and managed a bottle of decent claret. Having finished, he asked if he could have a look in the tiny kitchen, and Martin obliged. The following morning, Martin was on the phone to me to say that, without any doubt, he had been visited by a Michelin inspector the previous night. I was really happy for him until I asked what the inspector had drunk, and, on hearing that a bottle of claret had been downed, I questioned Martin a bit closer. There is no way that a Michelin inspector would ever do that, and neither of us was any the wiser until Chris returned and mentioned what a great dinner he had had in Leith.

It's a different story in Glasgow, however. Everyone knows how to have a good time there, and it's not thought irreligious to spend a few quid on proper wine. It's a more frenetic city, full of people who have no ambition other than to live life.

Just as we were discussing all this, the phone rang from Glasgow. Someone wanted to sell a big restaurant right in the heart of the city. We both went to look, and suddenly the old excitement resurfaced. Nothing thrills like the thought of a restaurant full of good food, good service and the musical whirr of the credit card machine. A million makeover versions swamped our minds. Everyone was writing their versions of the menu, sketching designs with seating plans on the back of used envelopes. The big question was: how far was the Rangers ground from there? How would it figure on a match day? I was dreaming, and already, in my stupid eagerness, I lost the plot.

Still, before I had time to think, the whole project had sprouted wings and suddenly there were surveyors, lawyers, electricians and rodent catchers, all present to put this together and submit fancy bills for their endeavours. I was getting a bit uneasy with the people who were selling the restaurant to us. They were keen – too keen – to impress me with the size of their other operations, and then suddenly they started to talk about the crappy abstract artwork in the restaurant. They pointed out that these early works of infants at school were not included in the sale, but could be made available as a side purchase.

Here we go again, I thought. However big someone is, Rule Number One is this: if there is cash, they want it, and these greedy arseholes were about to lose a deal because they wanted a few readies on top of a shedload of money for their restaurant.

Chris and I talked about it. We were both totally pissed off that, having talked through the heads of terms, some dickhead started to murmur about a few pictures so they could screw some more money out of us. We don't do side deals. So the deal turned stone cold, and Chris told them why. It no longer matters now, but they were totally mystified.

Then the phone rang. It was Glasgow again, and this time, One Devonshire Gardens, Glasgow's chic West End boutique hotel. Now this was a boner, and I was up there with Chris, as keen as a setter on the scent.

The place looked right immediately: three houses joined together and filled with browns, tweeds and long, elegant drapes, and with rooms the size of snooker halls. There was a smooth life going on here, but the one thing that they didn't have was a restaurant. Fuck me! We can arrange that. And, in doing so, fine dining would come to my home town. The more I saw of this fantastic establishment, the more I fell in love with it, and any numerical doubts faded away, along with my sense of judgement.

We went back to London, and the whole process of negotiation, lawyers and contracts started all over again. We found Scottish lawyers, who are a different bunch to our beloved Joelson Wilson & Co., but Scotland is Scotland, and they play by a whole different set of laws. Soon we had a deal, and it was only a matter of time before wet ink was scrawled across a ten-year lease and an accompanying operating agreement.

The first base in this home run, as always, was a chef, and I already knew who was going to head north to run the kitchen. This remote outpost would also need a general manager, and I had just the person in mind. From then on, there was a long succession of trips to One Devonshire

Gardens by our human resources manager, our operations staff and the kitchen designers. Gradually, a shape was evolving, and although the English press was pretty low-key about this adventure, the Scottish papers were lining up their sharpened pencils.

Amaryllis opened to a Scottish fanfare. We had a launch party that rocked late into the night, which was all very well, but the following day, we were open for business. The opening weeks went well. Nobody could believe that this restaurant was attracting forty covers for lunch and sixty-five in the evening. I did more television interviews and talked to more journalists than ever before. The critics moved in. Their reviews made good reading, and I knew we were already on the way to a Michelin star.

At what stage did I realize that things were going wrong and that the paste that held up the wallpaper was just too thin? Well, if the truth were known, it was not so for far too long.

But it was soon clear that the pressure from Glasgow on our London operation was beginning to grow. The northern kitchen brigade was rowing, absenteeism was at a level not known to us in the south. On top of all this, the owners of the hotel had just run into trouble.

It is always traumatic for everyone involved when there have to be changes in senior management. The finger of blame can only point to myself and Chris, and if we get an appointment wrong, then it will certainly be us who end up paying the price.

All you can do when you appoint someone is interview them and check out their reputation. But reputations are leaked, spread, smeared or openly published, and are often the stuff of crap and nonsense. I know how I can exaggerate and pass on stories about them as if I witnessed the whole thing myself – when, actually, I've never met them. As for the interview, well, that can be a trip to Disneyland. Nobody ever goes to an interview with a long list of their weaknesses. They save them for later, and drip-feed them when you least expect it.

So, a new appointment is made, and off we go into the woods, axes in hand, ready to build a tree house. All is sweet to begin with, and slowly, almost imperceptibly, ominous signs begin to appear. They may not have forgotten the axe, exactly, but, at some stage, it will need sharpening and the stone was left at home. The idea is that senior managers have to think things out for themselves. They have to plan, budget, foresee everything and make things happen. If you're building a tree house, you need drawings, materials, a compliant workforce, safety procedures to stop Bob the Builder from falling off the tree holding his chainsaw, and the house needs to face the right direction to catch the sun. In fact, someone must be experienced enough to see the whole thing through.

If that doesn't happen, you know you've got a problem. When a bend in the road appears, you get a choice. You can either steer around the corner or you can fail to notice it, ignore it, and crash. That's when you have the odious task of saying goodbye and having to look for someone else, and you know in your heart of hearts that it is not so much a senior management failure, but your own fucking fault – or Chris's fault, if I'm feeling that evil.

We were, as they say nowadays, ring-fenced from the hotel operation, which was now in the hands of receivers. In practice, that meant it was run by accountants whose only aim in life was to cream every penny out of this financial flop for the creditors, and that was never going to result in a well-run, happy hostelry with residents queuing up to sample my menu.

Still, we paid countless visits to *Amaryllis*. Chris and I would leave London at 4 a.m. and race up the motorway to be there by 8.30 a.m. When we got there, we would talk to staff, listen to their catalogue of woes, and then do the motivational bit, sure that – this time, finally – everything would change. I would gather all the poor, wee lost souls in the main dining room with the high ceiling and slight mustiness in the air, and I would talk gently. 'Guys,' I would say, 'we have some issues here that we need to sort out. We need to do this together, you and me, so that we can learn from our mistakes and make this so successful that the queue for dinner stretches right down to Sauchiehall Street. So tell me what you think might be wrong at present.'

Nothing is forthcoming, so I move it up a gear. I look for the face that shows that its owner wants to hide behind the drapes – those long, grey, funereal drapes that are looking more and more apt by the day – and I try and draw him out.

'Harry?' I ask. He's the barman who has personally ordered fifty-seven varieties of Scotch in the mistaken belief that he will entice most of Scotland into his bar. 'How are you with all of this? Do you feel that we can work this out as a team? What about you, Cynthia? How can we improve our daily reservations?'

And so I go on, asking and listening carefully. In their replies, the real answer is hidden. I need to hear the tone, the timbre and the inflection to see if they really think that this can work and to see – most importantly – if they *want* it to work.

I tell them that they are only here because they are good, and were chosen because of this attribute. I explain that London is not that far away, and that everyone in the office really wants them to succeed. Then I ask them if they can help me get the show on the road. And, bit by bit, I can see hope. They want this to work, and they know that I want it to do so as well. We can do it. We have the best fucking ingredients in the world on our doorstep. We need to spoil our guests with smiles and recognition. We need to deal with problems immediately, and always in favour of the customers. Are we together on this? The room tells me yes, and although it might be some way short of Billy Graham's call to Jesus, I really believe that I've encouraged them.

The trouble was that it never did change and, as this became apparent, we felt less like going up to *Amaryllis*, knowing that the love affair was over.

London was having its own problems by then. *Pétrus* had moved to The Berkeley and we had kept on 33 St James's.

It had seemed simple enough to give the restaurant a new name, make some changes to the menu, drop the prices fractionally, and wait for the same old crowd to keep coming. Only they didn't. Turnover plummeted, and we were suddenly no longer making £40,000 a month.

So Marcus Wareing and I were 'invited' to Chris's office for a chat. It was a bit like attending the funeral of the family pet. There, on his desk, he had sheets of paper with the past six months' profit and loss figures. We ploughed through them, starting with *Royal Hospital Road*, then on to *Pétrus* and the other restaurants we were beginning to open in London. They were bringing in total profits at the rate of around £250,000 each month, which was great.

'What was wrong with that?' we wondered, until Chris launched into a rundown on the two failing restaurants.

Marcus and I had a pocketful of reasons and excuses for this state of ruination, and, above all, we had the determination to fix it. There was a pause, and Chris said that he thought that we should shut the two restaurants the next day.

'Had he gone mad?' we asked.

Closing would be like admitting defeat, and, most importantly of all, how would it sound to the press?

There was another cold, stony pause from Chris before he delivered the well-aimed kick in the bollocks. 'You can continue on one condition,' he said, 'and that is that the two of you personally pay over to the company a total of £41,000 each month until you have everything under control and the restaurants are no longer bleeding the group dry.'

He went on to explain that both cases were past redemption and that, unless we were happy to carry these losses personally, say for the next six months at a cost of £366,000, he suggested that we spend the rest of the meeting planning the two closures.

It was really strange, but this was suddenly a moment of great clarity, and I felt a huge relief. Of course it was heartbreaking, but both Marcus and I, dumbarses that we were, knew that the game was up and we would no longer have to dread the monthly figures. We would just hear about profit without the big minus pulling at the rear.

Why didn't I see it before? It had to be vanity, and vanity – as I discovered – could be fucking expensive. But I had learned about the antidote: a bucket of cold reality and serious action if you want to avoid bleeding to death.

The only thing that I had to deal with was a loss of face in the Scottish press and a distant whisper about a small failure in London, but I was beginning to learn how to do that. Because, back in London, the biggest opportunity so far was about to fall into our laps.

CHAPTER FIVE

CLARIDGE'S

When you find a winner,
groom it daily.
Protect it with your life.

WHILE WE WERE battling with the problems in Glasgow, two things happened that suddenly shifted us into another gear. In January 2001, *Royal Hospital Road* received its third Michelin star. It was what I had been working my bollocks off for since I started in my first kitchen, and it broadcast to the world what we were about. It was also to bring the most important opportunity so far, as I was about to learn how to take on a major business challenge, rebuild it detail by detail, and then deal with success on a scale previously unknown to me.

Claridge's is one of the very few old-style, glamorous places that are the real thing. It has been open since before the Battle of Waterloo, and it was among the first establishments to introduce French cooking to Regency London. The Prince Regent had a permanent suite there. And it was from Claridge's, out of the blue, that we received another one of those phone calls with an invitation to talks about running its restaurant.

Ironically, Claridge's new owners, Blackstone Private Equity, had been the very people who had delayed the launch of *Royal Hospital Road*. I had no idea back then, of course, that they would come to be such an important part of my life.

From the moment I first heard of the idea, I knew that *Gordon Ramsay at Claridge's* was going to take us into a different league. The deal had everything and, in particular, a new word for me: 'synergy', the coming together of two bodies whose combined force would be greater than the sum of their parts. Claridge's from the history books, and me from a council house. Who would ever have thought it? I learned the significance of this little number rapidly.

The first hurdle was to get the new owners into believing that we could handle this operation. The man whom we negotiated with was John Ceriale, a name that would become iconic within Gordon Ramsay Holdings for years to come. I thought of him as a Bronx bruiser with an uncanny vision when it came to bringing old-fashioned, down-at-heel hotels into the twenty-first century. At this point in time, he had only been with Blackstone Private Equity for a year as their hotel real estate manager and had yet to make his name.

Chris got on particularly well with Ceriale. I think Ceriale saw me as the name above the door, whereas with Chris, he could see someone who could put in place a structure that would carry the whole operation. Their first meeting started with the question, 'Would Gordon be happy to do breakfast in his restaurant?' Chris is seated there with Ceriale and at least six of his 'advisors' and the senior management from Claridge's. The answer to the question was about to launch a relationship that, in the fullness of time, would provide Gordon Ramsay Holdings with an incredible billion pounds' worth of turnover in the coming years. A BILLION pounds. No firm in the world would turn that down, and we certainly weren't planning on stalling over a simple matter like breakfast.

Fortunately, Chris got the answer right. Without a second's hesitation, he said that that would be no problem and that Gordon would certainly be up for that, knowing full well that chefs just don't do breakfast. This had been the stumbling block for all previous contenders. How the fuck Chris imagined he was going to smooth this with me became the funniest thing he ever said. He just looked at me and said that, if it was going to be a problem for me, he would cook the breakfasts himself. Chris can't cook a breadcrumb.

The early days were difficult. It took an age before we finally got the nod, having been made acutely aware that I was probably the last in the line of those chefs whom Ceriale had invited to talks. Perhaps, understandably, he realized my reputation might not sit comfortably with Claridge's rearguard. There were certainly plenty of people who were ready to confirm that, and although they liked their eggs boiled, they didn't like the idea of them being 'fucking' boiled. I think what worked in our favour was that Ceriale was clearly a maverick and liked me. He had already realized that the rebirth of Claridge's was not a move to pander to the hotel's established clientele. What would happen when they were all dead and gone? What he had in mind was a rebirth of this old lady to accommodate the new money of a younger, wealthier generation. He sought to bring glamour by the bucketful, and he did so with top American designers and investment funds that no one had ever dreamed about.

Ceriale made it clear that, before we went any further, he wanted to meet me. He was one of those operators who was guided by his feelings about people. All his consultants were people he liked, and if we were going to secure Claridge's, he and I would have to connect. I guess that I am a bit like that myself. It is not easy to work with people you don't like, and it just so happens that I tend to like people who are good at their jobs. I think that it's also linked to the search for loyalty. You want to feel that someone is with you for a bigger reason than just a pay packet.

It was arranged for Chris to take John and the general manager of Claridge's to *Royal Hospital Road* for lunch, and afterwards, I would come into the dining room and meet them. It gave us a chance to show John what we were about. Impress him, maybe.

Lunch was a hard slog for Chris. The general manager, let's just call him GM as in General Motors – was clearly not on our side. He couldn't understand change, and yet was swept along by the energy and vision of his new boss. As Chris said, he had reached the pinnacle of hotel management and was now extending a very tentative toe into hotel realignment. But a step, perhaps, too far for him.

So these two pumped Chris for all he was worth during lunch, asking him all the questions and expressing their doubts about how I would appear as the spearhead for the new restaurant. Both Chris and I knew that I was, without doubt, the right choice, but, for the new owners, there were big bucks riding on the correct decision, so nothing was going to be decided there and then.

As I entered the dining room, I saw the three of them sitting in the corner. Chris did not look happy, and I was thinking that maybe things were not moving in the right direction. We all shook hands, and I could see at once why Chris was so impressed with John Ceriale. He is not tall, he is thinning on top to the point of balding, and he is straight out of the Mafia's family album. He was dressed immaculately, with blue suit, cufflinks on double cuffs, and a quiet tie. I wondered if I should be kissing his hand. 'Hey, Gordon, nice ta meet ya.' He told me that he enjoyed lunch and that he was hoping we might do some stuff together with Claridge's. He was definitely twitchy, and I saw his eye land on a waiter who had joined the company only a week before. 'Haven't I seen him before?' he asked. My heart sank, as I knew that we had snatched this boy from Claridge's. 'Have you been stealing my fuckin' staff, Gordon? Is this what you do over here? Is this how you operate?' The man was all over me, and I saw Chris shifting from one foot to the other like he was trying to run through a trough of honey. GM was also uncomfortable with the way the conversation was going. More like a good slapping than a conversation, I was thinking. GM was chewing his top lip like there was a sticky wart on it.

'If you don't like me, Gordon, I'm outta here. Do you want me to fuck off out of the restaurant?'

Jesus! What have I done here? I looked at him and it just came out. 'Yes, he came over from Claridge's,' – GM was looking on stonily – 'and he tells me that the staff have a picture of the new owners on their dartboard. He says that your head has the most holes in it. Why is that, John?'

He looked at me, and the whole of *Royal Hospital Road* had a frozen moment. 'Hey, is that so? They stick more darts in me than any other fella? Fucking brilliant.' And with that, he laughed aloud, grabbed my hand and shook it like we'd been the best of buddies for years. I wondered afterwards what prompted me to say that. It was pretty dangerous stuff, and I can only think that either I was getting angry with this man for talking to me in my restaurant as though I was a criminal, or I just wanted to show him that we could toss in the occasional Molotov as well.

Somehow, although I was not sure as they left immediately afterwards, I thought we had made progress.

Our deal was eventually struck, and we got control of the dining room and kitchen. Blackstone paid for the design and refit in return for 11 per cent of our turnover by way of rent. Maybe a high rent, but just look at what we were getting: a beautiful dining room in the heart of Mayfair with all the glitz that was about to come shimmering through the door. Even the kitchen fit-out was paid for, although we had to wade in and replan the whole area after what we considered was a muddled first attempt. In later deals, this became our area of expertise, but that's another story.

Within the old kitchen, there was a drink dispense area just opposite the main stoves where countless cocktails had been served to the waiting staff to take through to the dining room. It had been in my mind to look for a space to put in a chef's table, and this looked perfect. A chef's table was originally just a table in the kitchen for friends of the chef or visiting chefs who would sit down and taste the kitchen's offerings. This simple concept developed so that guests of the restaurant could also eat in the kitchen and learn more about what they were eating, about the ingredients and how they are cooked. Chris will always maintain that it was his idea, but the idea went up to the Claridge's management for their approval. They thought the concept hilarious, particularly the GM, and asked what we imagined the turnover generated by such a table of six would be. 'Probably around £440,000 a year,' Chris replied. They continued to laugh, but we got our way, and a year after opening it, had turned over £500,000 – probably more than Claridge's Royal Suite took in.

The Chef's Table became a trademark of our operation, and is a feature in nearly all of our restaurants. It makes great commercial sense. For years, guests never dreamed of coming near a commercial kitchen. Suddenly, everyone is interested – not just in food, but how it is put together, and its production has become theatre. The chefs love it when they see guests interested in what they do. Very often, they will invite the guests to the stove to help stir a pot or dice a shallot. The table is a great revenue source, and, occasionally, tips are exceptional – as once witnessed when the three ladies of a particularly lively Chef's Table stood up and bared their tits in gratitude. The brigade cheered and the evening became buried in folklore. Unfortunately, it was my day off.

The Chef's Table is also the guarantee of total hygiene. Everyone working in the kitchen knows that clean is not enough. It has to look as it did on the day it opened. Shine, polish, burnish, sparkle – the whole nine yards. No fucking excuses.

The opening of *Gordon Ramsay at Claridge's* was delayed by three months. It would have been inconceivable originally, but the combined noise of drilling and the preciousness expressed by hotel guests made the original opening date of July an impossibility. This had an unexpected benefit.

The taking over of Claridge's restaurant had brought to my attention the concept of TUPE, the Transfer of an Undertaking Protection of Employment. In essence, this meant that anyone employed by a going concern, company or business was automatically transferred as an employee to the new owners or employers, irrespective of how the transfer of the business took place. Sounds reasonable in the first instance – until you realize that you may be taking on employment liabilities relating to people with thirty years' service. In the case of Claridge's, there were something like eighty such employees, and this was a real concern. Not only had they been around this establishment for years, but during that time, they had taken on personas that would in no way suit the operation that we had in mind.

What I didn't realize was that they were as nervous about coming on board as I was about their existence. The easy life of serving twenty or so guests at lunch or dinner was about to come to an end. We were already working on 120 guests for lunch and 150 in the evenings, and word was out on what we expected from our staff. With this in mind, forty of the transferees had already tendered their notices and were on their way to pastures new or, perhaps, just out to pasture. With the announcement of a September opening, the others threw in the towel, every single one of them, and we were free to start afresh. Thank you, God.

For John Ceriale, there were always three fundamental components in opening a successful restaurant: the location, the chef and the design. Well, we certainly had the location, and the kitchen was never going to be a problem. The design – or, rather, the designer – was the ace up John Ceriale's sleeve. Tucked away in an old converted cold store in New York's Tribeca was Thierry Despont, who was given the commission to not only bring Claridge's foyer into the new age of old elegance, but was also charged with the design of my new restaurant.

Claridge's restaurant had been on the ground floor on the west side of the hotel for 100 years and had probably never turned a profit. It was a mausoleum – a huge, high-ceilinged cathedral where tail-coated waiters had pranced between the tables, dispensing arrogance and superciliousness while serving plates of grown-up school dinners. The task facing any designer would be daunting. It was easy to throw out the aspidistras and Victorian bric-à-brac, but all that was left was an echoing cave large enough to hangar a jumbo jet.

One winter's day, we found ourselves in Tribeca about to meet the man who was going to change all that. His cold store had been transformed into an amazing five floors of sample rooms, drawing desks and Apple Macs. He was a tall, nasal Frenchman with a confidence and arrogance that I liked. Moreover, he was someone who listened to us when we started on the long list of considerations that he would have to take on board. He presented a three-dimensional concept of what he had in mind. Fucking breathtaking, as we sat and watched. This was the guy who spruced up the Statue of Liberty on its 200th birthday, and now he was about to design my new restaurant.

You may remember that, earlier on, I thought that the Claridge's challenge was about to launch us into a different league and, in doing so, it would introduce me to a whole new world of international travel and an involvement with people who think in global terms. You know that I am already beginning to understand that this will become the template for the years to come, and I am shitting myself with excitement.

The deal to take this over was as simple as ABC. The owners were to pay all the big bills. The megabucks that were needed to make it happen came from them. All I had to do was find the money to supply the china, the silver, glassware, the 'tabletops', the staff uniforms, the kitchen equipment and a little working capital. I say 'a little working capital' because, of course, when the restaurant opened, money started to come in on the first night, even before the last table was crumbed down. That meant we had thirty days before we had to pay the staff and sixty days of income before having to pay a supplier. Chris, who had come from a thirty-year career in printing, reminded me that he had to wait between sixty and 120 days for his money in his previous life. The only thing that spoilt this positive cash flow arrangement was having to pay three months' rent in advance, provide a minimum of £100,000 in authorized and paid-up capital, and arrange a letter of credit from the bank to cover a quarter's rent in case of default. In addition, we paid 11 per cent of our net takings to Blackstone by way of rent. As I said, easy as ABC.

The negotiations over the drafting of the lease and the operating agreement went on forever. Chris spent hours in meetings with marked-up drafts going backwards and forwards. What we didn't realize then was that the format was to become a way of life for the two parties, and was to be used for a further twelve restaurants at the time of writing this. And that's simply because we got it right at the beginning.

The restaurant build seemed to take forever. It did, however, give us time to recruit the right staff, train them and make sure that everything was in place, ready for the big opening. It was time to acquaint ourselves with systems and procedures, which, in the coming two years, grew into Gordon Ramsay Holdings and set the stage for three new openings a year for the following five years.

The opening night was a glitzy affair – a real ball for all. The restaurant was cleared of tables and chairs so that over 500 guests could enter through the magnificent foyer of Claridge's to see the fabulous transformation of the mausoleum. Outside along the kerb were half a dozen nineteenth-century hackney carriages, each with a pair of horses with their noses in their feedbags – right back to when Claridge's first threw its doors open to the public. The press boys were everywhere, and even then, on that very first night, before the till had even rung up once, I knew that we had just broken through rock and found a vein of gold. John Ceriale, a shy man when it comes to the public, was there to see the launch of his baby with a grin the size of the Brooklyn Bridge.

That is not to say that *Gordon Ramsay at Claridge's* proceeded without a hitch. In the first year, we bottom-lined at £600,000. The second year was much the same. But in the third, we closed the year off at £1.65 million and then went on to reach close to £2 million in each successive year, and that must tell a tale.

The first year was hard. We were soon receiving, on average, sixteen letters of complaint a week, and something had to be done about it. The weekly operations meeting was born, which was no more than a meeting of the restaurant director, his managers, the head chef and his lieutenants, the head receptionist, the HQ heads of department from HR, training and private dining, and either Chris or myself to chair the meeting. They were often merciless meetings in our search for perfection. I recall one week when there were eighteen people all sitting in a large circle without a table to hide behind, and one of the receptionists, a fat, self-contented moose, smirked after admitting that she had lashed up on a booking. The smirk drained away as it was pointed out that, as she had risked jeopardizing the GR name with her recklessness, she could now leave the room, leave the company, and never be heard of again. And that is exactly what happened. Amazing, after that, how we had everyone's undivided attention.

So, what happened during the first two years that added a million pounds to the bottom line? Why did that not happen from the beginning? Surely there was a simple enough formula here of booking guests in from an apparently endless list of reservations requests, offering the same menu each day and washing the dirty plates at the end of each service. Most restaurants would have given their eye teeth to make £600,000 a year, but we knew that there was an opportunity to fine-tune every area of the operation, leading to bigger bucks and true longevity for the restaurant.

The single most effective step was to introduce profit and loss numbers to the kitchen management. Chefs are not normally numbers people, but I saw how they sat up when Chris alluded to the information that the office could pick up from the kitchen's activities just from the food margins, the primary indicator of how much was spent on ingredients, compared to the amount of food sales. If the chef carried on buying Welsh lamb when the prices went up without increasing the menu price or switching to Pyrenean lamb, his monthly food margin would drop a couple of points, and the office knew there was a fuck-up somewhere. The menu stayed more or less the same and, therefore, the food margins did not falter.

As the kitchens began to understand the importance of buying intelligently, turning stock and charging in accordance with market costs, a bonus system was introduced in accordance with performance. As such, it represented financial rewards for doing the job right. Commission or bonuses are nearly always associated with sales or deal making, and it just seemed right that safeguarding aspects of the bottom line also deserved reward and motivation to keep going along that track. This had to be carefully watched, as the last thing I wanted was overkill when margins rose at the expense of quality. That was not the idea. It's just that, when I think back to *Royal Hospital Road*, it was always our boast that we never bought on price, just quality and timely delivery.

The other essential indicator was salary costs as a percentage of sales. There had to be sufficient staffing, but not over-staffing. Also added into the formula had to be the training and retention of staff. When commis enlisted and then left in less than six months, we came up with a bonus system, whereby those staying for a year earned a one-off payment at the end of the term. This immediately had anyone thinking twice before throwing in the towel.

The art of upselling is a sensitive but necessary subject. There is nothing more irritating than when a table is approached half a dozen times and asked if they want water. Once is fine, and the question has to be asked. After that, it is vital that an indicator is left on the table so that any further approach is avoided. Either remove the water glasses if it was 'No,' or place a bottle coaster on the table to indicate that a bottle is already on the way. So simple.

Successful and intelligent upselling is bringing to the guests' attention something that they want, but just hadn't thought about. Sit a party down at the table and ask them what they may like to drink, and there will be total confusion. Particularly if the guests don't know each other. Suggest the champagne trolley, and you're home and dry. It cuts across the whole problem for a guest who doesn't want to be the first to choose. And, in the meantime, you kick off with six glasses of pink champagne on the bill at £9.50 a glass, with six happy guests who are beginning to realize that they are going to enjoy themselves.

Statistics on the *Gordon Ramsay at Claridge's* scale did my head in at the beginning. At Claridge's, we agreed to put £1 on every bill in the months of November and December for a London charity called StreetSmart. The proceeds were to go to London's down-and-outs, and we, in fact, decided to extend this to six of the restaurants. So, how much did £1 a table produce in those two months for six little restaurants? Something in the region of £23,000. That means that we served 23,000 tables – not guests – in sixty-one days. Extend this to the number of feet belonging to all the guests (allowing an average of two feet per guest) that make up these tables, and you begin to understand why we need a twenty-four-hour maintenance team, why we need to replace the fucking carpets every three years, and why, unless you do this, the place will wilt like a lettuce leaf at Ascot.

What do guests look for more than anything when entering a restaurant? What they want is attention. They want to see a smile, an acknowledgement, a welcome the moment they enter, and the average restaurant is fucking crap at this simple courtesy. Either you are completely ignored and staff at the reception desk carry on talking among themselves, or someone challenges you with 'Name?' And on giving your name, they repeat it like a fucking automaton, without so much as a 'Mr' or 'Mrs'. Their attention then flicks down the reservations list, and they proceed to highlight the name in Day-Glo green or rub it out like a gleeful schoolgirl, fresh from a shoplifting spree at Office World.

People in a restaurant see it as their chance for recognition. Give them a warm, welcoming smile. Get their name right with the appropriate title, and make it sound like you are really pleased to see them. They are already flushed pink that they are recognized and have your undivided attention. A good restaurant manager understands this, and ensures that his staff are drilled to follow these simple rules. For Christ's sake, the guests' satisfaction is what your job is all about. Get it wrong and you will hear no more because there won't be any guests left.

Once past the desk, the guest is now looking out for two things: which table he's going to get and whether any of the other guests are looking and thinking, 'a regular' or 'Who is this git who's getting the special stroking?' All part of the service, and still not a menu in sight.

So, in the early days of *Gordon Ramsay at Claridge's*, we decided to do something about the smile factor. I guess it stemmed from a remark that Chris made when he was asked what qualifications he had to run restaurants. He just looked up and said, 'I eat in them.' You see, what was going around in his maze of a brain was that chefs and waiters only see what they do from their own positions. They come through college, tiny kitchens and bistros, and never get to see the wider picture. I think it's called one-dimensional. So what I decided to do was invite our own staff to experience their own restaurant. Get done up, bring their nearest and dearest, and have a good time. They'll soon get pissed off if they are kept waiting for the main course or they have to pour their own wine or they have to try and understand what Zolga, the waitress from Latvia, is trying to say about the menu. It's an advanced education so that they actually know what it feels like when things go wrong. Why don't air crews get nervous when the wings on their planes flap hysterically in turbulence halfway across the Atlantic? They stay calm because they have been shown that the plane is built to survive, even when concrete blocks are dropped on it.

And that's what knowledge and understanding in *Gordon Ramsay at Claridge's* brought me. What we achieved as a team became an amazing success story. Ultimately, it depended on the little things like the smile people get when they come into our restaurants and the understanding of our guests' expectations gained first-hand by our staff. As ever, it is the detail that counts.

CHAPTER SIX

FOREIGN FIELDS

*Control from afar will bring its own
problems, and shouting from a thousand
miles away becomes but a whisper.*

By the end of 2000, my two London restaurants were running well. Mark Askew was looking after *Royal Hospital Road* in his usual brilliant and protective way, and Marcus Wareing was steering *Pétrus* into its second year of trading. It was a time for me to get bored or to look for something else – or somewhere else. I felt that somewhere there was a greater pulse to life, but I couldn't quite see how to grasp it.

What I was about to learn were the basic, underlying secrets of how to expand globally, with restaurants that were thousands of miles away. Same standards of cuisine, same standards of service, but with lines the length of which we had to extend control.

Then, just before Christmas that year, we had a call from Hilton asking if we might be interested in opening a restaurant in their new hotel in Dubai. It sounded a bit exotic, and both Chris and I were immediately all ears. This could be our first venture outside the UK, and, at the time, there were bucketfuls of hype about duty-free shopping malls and the unrelenting, bronzing sunshine of Dubai.

After a blitz of initial e-mails, we both agreed to go to Dubai straight after Christmas.

I have to say that, in those days, I never really got the hang of what Dubai was all about. Maybe you had to see it as a holiday resort where you just went and broiled yourself in the sun, but there seemed so little to do. Still, all we were doing was checking it out as a possible site to spread our wings.

We arrived on a Thursday in January 2001. This, actually, was treated in the Muslim world as a Saturday, and Friday became Sunday. Different culture, different calendar. I could cope with that, so what's next? Well, no stand-alone restaurants. All restaurants had to be in a hotel. Hmmm. OK.

We were picked up at the airport and taken to the Hilton Dubai Jumeirah, immediately learning Lesson One, that there were two lived-in parts of Dubai: the city itself and the resort area, with forty-five minutes of motorway between them. Our itinerary was full-on, even if Hilton hadn't quite got the hang of how to spell my name or, for that matter, the word 'itinery'. It was filled with presentations of the project, visits to half a dozen restaurants and a dazzling venture into the desert, riding a four-wheel wagon along the ridges of the dunes in the early evening and then stopping to watch the breathtaking sunset.

We were taken for lunch in a submarine to the seafood restaurant within the Burj Al Arab and then shown around this towering monument to the future of Dubai. The submarine, of course, didn't move, and when I went into the restaurant, with its wrap-around fish tank, I began to realize that I had entered a Disneyland for crustaceans. I can't even remember what the food tasted like, and I guess that most people left with the same experience.

The hotel was just a building site in the city next to the Dubai Creek. It was also the first building I had ever been in while it was being built. It is so difficult to visualize a bar area or the entrance to your restaurant when all you see in front of you is raw concrete and piles of sand, tiles and hard hats. But I couldn't help being impressed. It was to become a beautiful steel and glass boutique hotel, probably not in the best position for the Dubai tourist, but graceful and upmarket.

But when we went on an early morning visit to the fish market it was a different story – and a frightening experience for the prospect of doing business there. The heat was fucking incessant, and there was all this fish lying around in the least hygienic environment imaginable. Great slabs of tuna weighing 200 pounds were left for an hour on the tarmac of the access road while someone went off to get the truck. The place was a fucking shambles, and I was glad to move out of the smelly, dirty sales halls. The thought of coming down to market in the early morning to buy the day's fish supplies for the hotel didn't give me a rush of confidence. Here, for sure, was a clash of the old Arab culture and today's new hotel culture, with all its Western expectations.

Nor was the welcome from the owners exactly over-whelming. This was going to be a three-way deal between them, Hilton as the operators, and us for the food and beverage consultancy. So, I guess, in the owners' minds, we were just a Western name that had to be imported. They would have little control over us, so we were an irritating necessity that had to be tolerated.

It struck me then, as it has many times since, that hotel operators around the developing world have to adapt them-selves to a million different cultures. I have met one or two senior hotel people who do nothing but act as diplomats, easing the relationships between operators and owners. I always think of it as a hard way to earn money.

After all that, the trip was a success. We left Dubai agree-ing to move forward, and the deal was relatively simple. We would license the name of Gordon Ramsay to Hilton for its use in anything to do with promoting food and drinks in the hotel. We would also supply ten senior staff members and the menus, and be consultants about food and drink. All that was left was for Hilton to come over to London, with the owners' representatives, so that we could show them we were the right choice.

But there was an immediate problem. We could hardly sail into our shoebox office in the Fulham Road with our guests and announce that this was our headquarters. Not much commercial cred there. So, Chris's sitting room in Mayfair, with its enormous oak table, had to become our central office. Miraculously, it worked. By the time they had been to the restaurants and listened to Chris's spiel, we were in, and they were happy to start the legal process. Looking back now, it was probably the last time we had to puff out our cheeks to make ourselves look bigger than we were.

In the following months, we did everything necessary to get the the hotel ready for its opening. We had already decided on Angela Hartnett to lead the team in Dubai. She would leave our employment and join Hilton for a two-year tour. This was an inspired choice because Angela was so much more than just a chef. She could organize and motivate people and still remain the beautiful survivor of the *Aubergine* days. No one could resist her charming manner, and I always knew that our name in Dubai would be safe.

Towards the autumn, the hotel began to open. I say 'began' because that's how it was. First, the foyer and a few floors were open to the public. Then the food and beverage operation kicked in, and, gradually, the show hit the road. That is, until the fateful date of 11 September 2001. This was to guarantee an almost empty hotel for weeks to come. Suddenly, nobody wanted to go near the Middle East.

It was a bit like John West tinned salmon and Perrier water. They both collided with commercial reality, but memories faded a little bit with each dawn. It just needed the rawness of what happened to blur a little, and then things began to return to how they were – or in our case, how they were meant to be.

The one thing that we, as restaurateurs, hadn't yet experienced was the difficulty of dealing with problems so far away. If something flares up in Mayfair or St James's, we can be there in ten minutes. Not so when your restaurant is thousands of miles away, in a different time zone and, for that matter, on different days of the week. What's more, we were already dealing with the beginnings of *Gordon Ramsay at Claridge's* and the end of our first Scottish adventure. Somehow we had to hold it together, and deal with Dubai at a distance.

The early problems were about hiring and keeping staff when they were far more used to our salary scales than the budget-driven rates of Hilton employees. That was when we started to do something really stupid. To keep our people there to protect our name and promote all things Gordon Ramsay, we started to pay them a supplement from London. Apart from our signing-on fee, all we got was a flat percentage of the monthly food and beverage turnover. After 9/11, this revenue stream was so thin that our staff supplements were gobbling up the whole lot.

Worse, our main restaurant – which we called *Verre* – was short of most of the elements that go into a restaurant for fine dining. Chris went over a number of times and would leave pages of notes on how to turn this around. Most of all, he begged for a carpet. It was perfectly clear that the wooden floor, glass wall and absence of any drapes or soft furnishings needed a rethink. Quite apart from anything else, the quietest conversation would echo around the room. A carpet would have been a good start, but a year passed ... and still no carpet.

It was so difficult for Hilton to persuade the owners to respond that I began to think that this wasn't about running a decent restaurant or hotel, but some private battle of wills. Or maybe the owners just decided to do it in their own time. For some bizarre reason, we were never allowed to contact the owners directly. This was their rule, not Hilton's, and it was the one and only agreement we ever had where we never got to speak to our partners.

I'll say one thing for Hilton. They were always tied to their budgets and hotel culture, but they were sometimes capable of thinking outside the box. Chris explained that, if they insisted on giving tiny rooms to the Gordon Ramsay inmates and salaries to match, there would soon be no staff worth having. They agreed to tear up the agreement – or, at least, rewrite the relevant clauses. At last, we were able to drop our salary supplements. Even a new carpet threatened to happen, and solutions to all the changes that we had whinged about. Finally, and it was an enormous fucking relief, *Gordon Ramsay at the Hilton Dubai Creek* began to take off. Both parties had acted like grown-ups and, at last, we were marching on together.

We have never made much money in Dubai. There have been regular revenues fed over to us and paid in what must be the world's weakest currency, the US dollar. But the one message that came loud and clear was that a lot of the guests who came to our London restaurants also visited *Verre* in Dubai. They go there, I think, because they feel that they can rely on the quality and the standard. It repeatedly won *Time Out Dubai*'s Restaurant of the Year, and was clearly rated as the pinnacle of cuisine in the city.

Angela came through her two years like a shining star. Her rapport and loyalty with the staff were legendary, and she was able to keep her head in a crisis. Sometimes, the crises were extreme. After one successful Christmas, she organized an evening on a barge in the creek with a buffet and dance for all the staff. As she sat next to her senior sous-chef at the stern of the rusting tub, the handrail gave way, and both plunged into the black waters. By the time they were fished out, the sous-chef was dead. This was like the loss of a family member, and yet, the following morning, Angela was back in her kitchen and there for her staff when they needed her.

By then, things were happening in London, and we were putting together ideas for *The Connaught*. Angela was brought back to take charge. She had proved her worth many times over, and now it was time to reward her work with a new operation and a small stake in the equity. She had also brought on her Dubai successor in the person of Jason Atherton, who, in time, would cut his teeth there and return to London to open *maze*, a groundbreaking new restaurant that was to bring him to the forefront of the rising stars.

If running top restaurants around the world simultaneously was the problem, this was our solution, and it was the exact opposite of my press caricature as an uncontrollable boss, shouting and swearing at the staff. It was all about finding the best people and making sure we kept them. Everything we do depends on loyal staff on whom we can rely.

Finding great talent, looking after staff and nurturing their talent is what we learned to do well. Losing good people is symptomatic of only one thing: truly crap, appalling and abysmal management.

It also meant that I didn't have to be there in person so much. My visits to Dubai were supposed to take place four times a year. This was no great problem in the early days, but it gradually decreased to two visits, as the pressure on my diary grew elsewhere. In the meantime, the city of Dubai was also growing like a fucking monster. I remember, on my first visit, how someone had pointed along a road where there were three hotels and told me that eighteen more were being built there. Five years later, there were close to 100 hotels going up. No wonder I kept hearing that 27 per cent of the world's cranes were there, on a million building sites.

Once we had sorted the initial problems, all our staff who went out for a two-year tour enjoyed life there. It's tax-free, of course, and there is plenty of free time to improve your golf handicap. Jason Atherton not only got his down to scratch, but also found the time to acquire a beautiful wife.

That is jumping ahead in the story. By the time Dubai was beginning to run smoothly, we had made the leap – in little more than a year – from being a very successful oper-ator of two small London restaurants to being a global group. That brought challenges of its own and, for me, an urgent lesson that was absolutely fucking vital. I had to learn what to do when we got complaints – and the hidden benefits of people complaining.

CHAPTER SEVEN

WE WRITE TO TELL YOU HOW DISAPPOINTED WE WERE

You are never always right, and in your customer's view, you are probably wrong. Sometimes it's best to give them the benefit of the doubt.

IN THE *AUBERGINE* days, I had become an arrogant little fucker, and whenever a letter of complaint arrived, it went straight in the bin as an appropriate testimony to the writer's credentials. When we started at *Royal Hospital Road*, this tradition carried on. It seemed normal enough, until one day Chris found out and came storming into the restaurant to point out a couple of home truths. Fuck! He can rant when so moved. And what pissed me off, of course, was that he was bang on the button.

He went on about binning the most valuable management tool in the chest, not to mention a page from the guest services' bible. I always grit my teeth when Chris's face starts to turn puce. You know you're in for a bollocking and a lecture, but you just fear the bastard is going to have a heart attack before he delivers the point. On this occasion, he went on about how one stone thrown in the pond causes ripples from the centre to the edges and you can't stop them, and how important words like humility, feedback, reputation and word of mouth are if we want to be serious restaurateurs. A guest has gone to *Gordon Ramsay* and has, of course, told friends, family and half of fucking Islington that he (or she) is going. So, the next time he sees everyone, they ask what it was like. If the reply comes back 'Crap,' the ripples have reached the edge of the pond. Time to launch the lifeboat. So spake Chris. He cooled down, and we then changed our policy.

The letter of complaint is the one chance to do two things. I now know this.

The first move is to read it and work out what sort of letter we have here. Has this guest who has bothered to write got a genuine point, or is he just whingeing? Was he kept waiting for forty minutes for the menu? Did the sommelier sound sniffy when asked for table water? Was someone ironing a tablecloth in view at 4.30 p.m., ready for the evening service? Or is this letter so vitriolic about every aspect of dinner that you might begin to suspect that this is an arsehole looking for a freebie?

What we need to know is whether or not we did something really stupid, and can we improve ourselves? Is there some blemish that has gone unnoticed until now? It is important for us to take a step back and look at the complaint with objectivity. Although it is vital to redeem our name with a guest when things go wrong, it is also of paramount importance that we analyse what went wrong and learn from it. You cannot do that if you are being sniffy and precious about the complaint.

The second move is to deal with the complaint. If a scarf has been lost because we gave it away to someone else, then it's our fault. We mustn't concern ourselves that there is now someone waddling around with a shatouche scarf around his neck that he knows isn't his. Take it on the chin and write a cheque. If the waiter got muddled and refilled a still water glass with sparkling water, then apologize and make it perfectly clear that, on their next visit, the guest's table will be welcomed with a glass of champagne. We tripped up on our own shoelace, and this is the cost.

The big complaint, where clearly everything went tits-up, is different altogether. Not only do we start by apologizing without proffering any kind of excuse, but we make it clear that we are already in debt to the guest for bothering to write and tell us about whatever ghastly fuck-up took place. An apology removes the wasp's sting and prepares the wound for suitable medical attention. Start giving reasons for why it went wrong, and you are challenging the guest. This is not the time, believe me. The ruffled feathers need stroking back into some semblance of order.

Once we are into the fourth paragraph of apologies, self-flagellation and the Opus Dei treatment, we deliver the *coup de grâce*. We invite the table back as guests of *Gordon*

Ramsay, which will give us the opportunity to redeem ourselves. The only slight brake on kissing the wasp's sting better is the phrase 'with wines chosen by our sommelier'. We are happy to gild the lily, but we are not turning it into a pot of gold.

So, back to the pond. The guests return and have a swell time. The front of house performs miracle surgery, and the guests who arrive with a certain apprehension suddenly realize that we are serious about this act of redemption. The wasp's sting heals, and before you know it, a letter arrives saying, 'Fuck me, that's better.' And guess what? The fifty people they told previously about the crap time are now hearing that it was all put right. A happy ending and a result that was never anticipated. It is, believe me, the one and only way to deal with a serious complaint.

So, the moral is never to be so much up your own arse that you cannot say sorry. That and the welcoming smile can do as much to keep guests onside as anything that comes out of the kitchen. You have set yourself up to be the best experience in town and, as in real life, your real test is when the train comes off the rails. When someone has a problem, they want to know that the perpetrator is getting things back on track.

There is a final thought attached to this gruesome scenario. You only know things went wrong because the guest wrote a letter. My guess is that only three people in ten would bother writing. The other seven just don't come back. So the real answer is to get it right first time round. Smooth seas don't require lifeboats.

CHAPTER EIGHT

THE CONNAUGHT

*From the excitement of an idea through to
completion of the new project, give it
your full attention. Then leave it to
others to look after.*

GORDON RAMSAY AT CLARIDGE'S was open and proving a
total success. The monthly figures proved that, and Blackstone
were feeling pretty good about this. So much so that John
Ceriale decided to organize a PR event for the Savoy Group
in New York. While everyone was over there, he arranged a
dinner party at his home in Connecticut and invited Chris and
myself along. Frankly, we had so much on that it would have
to be a very quick trip, and Chris, who hates spending big
money on first-class travel, suggested that we go Air India.

'It's not only comfortable and half the price of our flag
carriers, but the food is amazing,' he told me.

On later trips I put my foot down, but right now, I looked
and listened with patience and angst.

The following week, having pitched up at the Air India
desk at Heathrow's Terminal 3, we handed over our pass-
ports to a big-haired woman at the desk who, after studying them, gave a strange look and asked which of us was

the woman. I looked at Chris, he looked at me and we requested a repeat of the question. She leaned over and showed us a picture from the passport of Greta, Chris's wife. In his rush, he had picked up the wrong passport. I remember thinking: thank God it wasn't me. He never gets things like this wrong, but that day, he scored a fucking bullseye. He called Greta and asked her to get the Paddington Express with his passport, and hopefully she would arrive in time to get him on the plane.

We were already under pressure because when we got into New York, we would have to shoot over to Grand Central, find the right train and get up to Connecticut. If we missed this plane, we wouldn't get to Ceriale's party, and I already knew that Chris needed to get there. He had a plot, and this was a threat to his scheme. While we waited for Greta, Chris quietly moved over to the Virgin desk and found that there was a later flight to JFK. He booked a one-way ticket in case Greta didn't arrive in time and I had to leave without him. I saw that he used his own credit card.

The passport arrived in time and we got on Air India, bound for JFK. Not only was the price low, but the lunch trolley was amazing and the service and comfort were all excellent, just as Chris had said, but I knew that I wouldn't be travelling that way again. Why? Maybe it was the Bollywood films that put me off, but perhaps now is the time to be a bit more honest with myself. Why was I turning my nose up at this carrier? The truth is that I sometimes miss being famous. As simple as that. If I go Virgin Upper

Class, I am recognized and I get looked after. With Air India, I am not known, and I just miss the buzz that comes with air travel. How sad is that?

The trip up to Ceriale's house in Westport was on a commuter train at the end of the afternoon. This is how New York workers come and go to work – no different from London, with the same overcrowded, dirty trains. I remember how, a couple of years later, I was in New York with Ceriale, and I asked him if he gets back home on the same train when it's late at night. He smiled and, with his left hand on my shoulder, leaned over and whispered that those days were long since over. He had become rich and had moved into the world of limos and private jets. You can't forget moments like that.

We arrived on an incredibly warm evening. The house was, as expected, big and beautiful in the American way, and situated in one of the most expensive real estate areas on the eastern seaboard. Everyone was drinking ice-cold pink champagne and, as though they had all been waiting for us, we went straight into dinner. There were two tables, and I was on the fun one. Chris, I noticed, was not only on the other one, but seated between John and his head money guy, Bill Stein. I hoped that he had remembered his script, though, somehow, I didn't think he'd need it. He had heard that John was in London at The Connaught the previous week and was showing around a well-known chef from Chicago. If The Connaught was up for grabs, then we wanted it, and this was a perfect time to say so.

The evening came and went. Everyone was in high spirits, and since all the guests were from the Savoy Group or Blackstone, their behaviour leaned towards the formal, as they were being entertained by their boss. Pierre Koffmann had been included, as *La Tante Claire* was still very much in The Berkeley, and the various general managers from each of the hotels were present, ready for their PR assault on New York the following day. Later on, we were in a limo on our way back to New York, and I asked Chris how he got on.

'I think they want to talk to us about The Connaught,' was the only reply.

Chris, as usual, had gone straight to the point and asked what they had in mind for The Connaught. They were, at first, surprised that we would be interested, and promised to come to London in the next two weeks to discuss a possible way forward. How exciting was that? We were fresh from our Claridge's success and feeling that little or nothing could go wrong.

Two weeks later, we met up in one of the quaint, tiny suites in The Connaught with John Ceriale and his band of merry men. It soon became apparent that we were not going to be allowed to stroll in, take up the food and beverage operation of this hotel as though we were entitled to it, and disappear into Money Valley. Nothing is that easy. What they wanted was *Royal Hospital Road*. They had it in mind that we could close the Chelsea operation and move it lock, stock and barrel into the hotel. That was never going to happen. *Royal Hospital Road* is my longstop in the event that all goes tits-up in my commercial life. It's there to provide me with a living, no matter what happens, and it certainly wasn't going to be transferred to The Connaught, however much we wanted this new operation. The Blackstone boys didn't take well to this at first. As John had said, there had to be something special here. It was not just a question of opening a restaurant and carrying on in the same old way, feeding an established clientele with the same old goo that they had been eating since 1897, when the hotel was built.

Ceriale asked for inspiration, something different. What about a woman chef? Did we know any? Like Nancy Oaks, who has *Boulevard* on the West Coast. We were acquainted with her from our work with Singapore Airlines. I knew exactly what was coming next from Chris.

'Funny you should say that, John. We have exactly the right person. When do you want to meet her?'

John's eyes narrowed, and he was quickly reassured that we might have the answer.

The meeting disbanded and we agreed to meet again in a fortnight, complete with our woman chef. The question was: how could we get Angela Hartnett, who was still running Dubai, to think the same way? She would freak. In Dubai, she had complete control. Why interfere with such a comfortable life to come over and be faced with all The Connaught's complexities? Somehow, we had to work on her – big time.

Angela is beautiful, funny, entertaining and freezes the balls off most men. She's not domineering in the slightest, but just has this ability to terrify. She's also the type who does it her way – no face-pack and three hours with the beautician before a critical meeting. Jokes of taking her down to the car wash are cracked at your own peril. We asked her to come over for this preliminary meeting and see what would happen, and this she agreed to. The meeting was set.

The morning of the meeting was fucking fraught. If this went wrong, we not only stood the chance of losing the prize, but we would have the added frustration of seeing someone else operating on our own doorstep. Angela arranged to meet Chris downstairs. It had already been decided that I wouldn't be present, as the spotlight had to shine 100 per cent on her. She appeared, as cool as you like, with a slash of red lipstick and her hair let loose. They walked upstairs to the meeting, and I later heard that all the foyer staff were watching. The bastards knew what was happening, and they were desperately hoping that we would fall flat on our noses. As the intrepid two entered the room, Chris saw that John had brought everyone to the show, his advisors and the Savoy Group GMs, and there they all were, sitting around with their teacups and extended little fingers. Angela simply said, 'Good morning, gentlemen,' and sat down in an armchair, full-on to Ceriale. She looked dazzling in a Pre-Raphaelite way – red hair, red lips and a beauty that Ceriale could not miss. The meeting started.

John likes women. You could tell he was immediately drawn to our Angela. They began with a few niceties, and within five minutes, Chris knew that he was superfluous. The GMs and advisors, the eavesdropping waiters and any mice that might be scavenging around for a few bread-crumbs were all out of it. These two were in serious, deep conversation, and we need never have worried. With a name like Ceriale and with Angela being half-Italian, the two were made for each other.

The meeting adjourned, and John called Chris aside.

'This broad is fucking perfect. We're there. I'll get Bill to start drawing up the papers.'

And he was off. No need to discuss the matter any further, and, as he left, there was a clank of china, as every-one rushed to put their teacups down and follow *il Maestro*. It was like an Italian court scene from an earlier century.

The differences between The Connaught and Claridge's are many. In fact, it is easier to look at their similarities, namely the fact that they are both Mayfair hotels owned by the same people. From that point on, they diverge in their clientele, their sizes and their appeal, and here we were taking them on as though we had been doing this all our lives.

The root problem with the food and beverage in The Connaught is that it all has to come out of the same kitchen. In Claridge's, there are two kitchens: one for our operation, and a lower, basement kitchen, where the hotel can accom-modate room service, a ballroom and private dining. What these two separate kitchens do is cater for two completely different cultures: the restaurant operator and the hotel operator. What is it that divides the two? The restaurant chefs cook for guests who have come simply to eat. All the sideshows of a beautiful room, a swanky address, precious design and white linen are just that. If the food is no good, then the restaurant will close sooner, rather than later. The hotel kitchen brigade, on the other hand, is ancillary to a hotel guest's experience. That guest has come because the hotel provides the room that he wants, and with it will come its own collection of sideshows including, somewhere, a kitchen. These additions are all important, but the centre of focus is not on food supply, which is just one of many boxes to tick.

This was the single biggest realization when Blackstone arrived. They knew that a good restaurant could make all the difference to a hotel, and for that to happen, there had to be an independent operator. It is the one reason why the world's hotels suddenly offered a marketplace to global restaurant brands, with Joël Robuchon's *L'Atelier*, Alain Ducasse's *Spoon* and Jean-Georges Vongerichten's *Vong*.

With the one kitchen in The Connaught there was no choice but to hand it over to the restaurant operator, Angela Hartnett, on the condition that she handled the entire food and beverage requirements for the hotel.

The logistics were immense. This was a hotel that needed massive change, but it had to be done very carefully. It was not like Claridge's, where you were looking for a whole new clientele. This needed smaller changes, such as getting rid of the *ancien régime* of the existing French kitchen and its funeral parlour of a dining room. This was where lamb chops at £30 were roasted way past pink in the kitchen, taken upstairs by an undertaker in black tails, and then recooked on a Bunsen burner in the dining room until every bit of young, sweet Welsh lamb had been incinerated and passed on to its maker. This was a dining room where a table of four could have seventy separate items on the table before dinner was even served, and stuck right in the midst of these tables was a vast mahogany service island, full of spirit lamps, empty silver dishes and piled-up dirty plates. There was a continuous clatter to accompany this merry scene, as old men dressed in the depressing black of their trade did their best to look aloof as they shovelled potatoes and tired-looking French beans from one dish to a waiting plate. You knew they just needed to complete their thirty-minute tour of duty before disappearing into one of the kitchen recesses for a life-sustaining fag or swig of gin. Fuck me, there had to be some changes.

For the first six months, we were open only half-cock. The main restaurant had closed for refurbishment, and many of the rooms were being redecorated as the public areas were undergoing a facelift. The regular guests were keeping away. Their idea of The Connaught was peace and privacy – without the dulcet tones of a jackhammer. It gave Angela a chance to organize some of the other areas, including the staff restaurant, room service and bar. The only trouble was that the revenue streams were thin, and from the first month, we were sustaining huge losses. Confident that, at the end of six months, we would emerge into the sunshine of profit, Angela battled on. Did she but know it then, two whole years would pass before red became black and *Angela Hartnett at The Connaught* would start to make money. But we didn't know that then. We thought we just needed to wait for the restaurant to be finished.

The kitchen needed a total rip-out. It was filthy, vile and should have been closed years before. What was once a beautiful Rorgue stove was now a grease-encrusted sinking battleship with a split across its upper deck where kitchen porters had been allowed to throw buckets of cold water at the end of service. This was the chef's idea of cleaning a kitchen – cold water on a hot stove. Expansion, contraction and ruination. As the stove was taken to pieces and trundled out by the scrap metal boys, there on the floor, as comfortable as any little home, was a rat's nest.

Adjoining the kitchen was the chef's office, full of crap and a testament to a different, long-gone era. It was here in the evenings after service that the senior staff were wined and dined by their own staff at the hotel's expense, and it was here that members of the royal family would drop in to say hi to everyone after dinner. I bet they didn't get introduced to the rats.

The jackhammer moved in and the cracked, cream floor tiles were uprooted like rotting teeth from a giant, while the white lavatory wall ceramics were split into a million little pieces and bagged up, ready for their next life as hard core. The place was a labyrinth of corridors and small cells of kitchen memorabilia. There was the silver room, where electroplated nickel silver was replated and burnished, ready for the upstairs dining tables, and adjoining that was the staff canteen and kitchen. Like a fifties' coffee bar, it was where the staff would unfold their *Suns* and *Mirrors*, light up the day's twentieth cigarette, and look wryly at the tray in front of them with its beans, chips, fried egg and doorstep of bread and margarine. They would be assessing the day's gossip and extending their breaks to breaking point before grudgingly moving off to their own areas of expertise and cosy chats with the housekeeping staff. But the mood had always been genial, with no real understanding of pressure until I arrived. I saw that I was viewed as someone who had fallen through the pavement grating and arrived there by some ghastly mistake. I was seen as the end of an era, a time that everyone dreaded, but knew would arrive one day.

Gradually, a huge, empty void was all that was left of the kitchen areas. The smell of dry concrete dust was everywhere, and the wet trades moved in to lay the tiles that would become the face and floor of Angela Hartnett's new kitchen. Within three weeks, the new stoves arrived from France, with gleaming chrome panels that promised to heat a million copper saucepans. These beautiful ranges would be rewarded with a twice-daily clean and polish. No lazy, bone idle cold water rinses in our kitchens.

The walls filled up with glass-fronted fridges, and a vast canopy installation curved down from the ceiling to suck away the heat and smells, ready for new air. It was hard, at this point, to see how food would ever be produced here. It was still a building site, and it would be Angela's job to transform it into the most comprehensive, dynamic kitchen I had experienced. *Claridge's* was the first super-kitchen, and now we have *The Connaught*, showing how a very busy restaurant needs a kitchen with space for twenty cooks to work without slicing each other's fingers to the bone. I thought back to the dark old days of Paris, where a brigade of six chefs worked in an area two metres squared, and yet turned out the most amazing, creative dishes. That was not the way forward. Times had changed, and there was a much, much better understanding of space and what could be done to maximize it. Get the kitchen wrong, and you will have a lifetime of rowing at the pass, of forgotten dishes and fucked-up cooks who begin to wonder why they ever walked into a kitchen. This was our chance to make our kitchens the work areas of serious, creative minds, where guests were welcomed and not denied entry. A kitchen has to be there for all to see, inspect and then enjoy. You know it's working when guests want to pick up a ladle and stir or chop chives at the side, and be part of this theatre.

In the meantime, the workmen slowly put together what we had planned over the months. The workflows had been designed so that plates on their way out don't collide with the plates on their way in. The 'plonge', or plate washing area, is filled with a conveyor belt that pulls plates along into the eighty-degree sousing, while the pot wash is worked relentlessly by kitchen porters at the bottom rung of the tall, tall ladder that may, one day, lead to the stove. There is a steep staircase leading directly from the kitchens up to the dining room entrance. It is a two-lane highway – the left side for down traffic, the right for up traffic, and had to be built for a heavy, daily pounding. The down side had to be more durable. Just watch waiters fly down for their next loads, compared to their much more deliberate ascents with trays laden with plates ready for the table.

Above you, the corridors are heavily networked with miles of wiring and pipework. This is the clever route for, once installed, everything is covered with a false ceiling and access hatches for maintenance. Out of the way and yet accessible. Right now, there was chaos that nobody in their right mind could ever see as part of what we were trying to build. There was no urgency, and it was fucking hard not to start shouting and waking everyone up from their trance. I needed the kitchen finished. I needed the dining room open. Every closed day was costing money, and here were the builders slopping around between tea breaks, doing so little – or so it seemed. But I was desperate for the instant action and energy that belongs to a kitchen, and if I stopped to think about it, that was not how electricians, painters and plumbers went about their business. I was at the mercy of a workforce that I had no experience of, and it was probably best that I just keep away.

Eventually (and weeks late), the kitchen was handed over. No champagne launch at the edge of the slipway, just an igniting of the stoves, a flood of white light as all the overhead lamps came on, and the growing hum of the air supply. For a moment, all the cooks were dazzled, frozen for that second before exploding into action, unpacking supplies, filling shelves and bringing this kitchen to life. The following day, it began to smell like a kitchen, as the stock-pots steamed and the first offerings came out of the ovens. There would be a week of sea trials before any dining room was filled with hungry guests, and it was during this week that the brigade would begin to understand this kitchen and the new menu that Angela had drafted, tasted and refined over the previous weeks.

If builders have their own pace of life, it is like a fast track, compared to that of the interior designer. Waltzing around with drawings and samples, explaining to anyone with ears how a warmth will exude from a three-centimetre square of fabric that has just come over from Germany and is impregnated with rich silk strands is not my idea of getting on with it, of getting the job done. The ceiling of the dining room was a beautiful cast of Victorian-style wedding cake, and no one could quite agree on the degree of off-whiteness needed to make it serene and comfortable. Fuck me. Did they honestly think that guests were going to put their knives and forks down and ponder this overhead dilemma? Detail is all very well, and a vital element in its place, but anyone who has painted their front room knows that while the paint is drying, you fret about a stray hair from the paintbrush that has somehow escaped and embedded itself on the ceiling. Within a week, it will have become invisible and forgotten.

Far better for this interior designer to have concentrated on the longevity of what might or might not look pretty. We would have to live with whatever he concocted from his store of three-centimetre samples, long after he had received and probably spent his exorbitant fee. Carpets need to have a long life. They are abused from Day One, when feet bring in everything that has been discarded on to the pavements of London by smokers, dogs and gum chewers. People with big feet, big feet carrying heavy people, and the six-foot chicks who turn their six-inch heels on a sixpence and screw the pile of the 'commercial' grade carpet into a tuft cannot be asked to remove their shoes before eating. It's just not the thing in London. Dirty carpets need industrial cleaning, and that means revolving scrubbing brushes and the type of detergent that has the power to clean off elephant poo. In short, the carpet has to last through all this abuse long enough to make reasonable commercial sense without looking like the left ear of a wet wolfhound. How long is 'commercial'? Three years? Every 150,000 people? Well, we found out the hard way. After only eleven months, a call to complain to the carpet supplier was met with a 'number unobtainable'. He had gone up the Swanee, along with our year's guarantee.

Then came the day when everything was suddenly finished. The hotel was open in all its glory, and we had a launch party. This wasn't like our opening at *Claridge's* where there was unlimited room for the partygoers. It was a crush, and somewhere, someone was trying to launch a book amid this throng. It paid for the champagne and canapés, and brought in a set of people that wouldn't normally have been on our invitation list. Angela arrived late, but in a beautiful red dress, and she looked radiant and happy. She finally had real guests and a business to run. The invitations had specified 6.30 p.m. to 9 p.m., and at 8.50 p.m., no one had moved. It was like sale time at Harrods, except here, everyone had a glass in their hand. There was only one way to clear the place so that we could prepare for the next morning: cut the booze. The waiters with the free-flowing bottles of bubbly were withdrawn, and within twenty minutes, we had our hotel back. We inspected the damage: a few cigarette butts stamped out in the carpets, one black hole burned into the seat of a banquette in the Red Room, but otherwise, not too bad. Aren't people wonderful?

Outside we had used a pantechnicon, full of the restaurant's tables and chairs, as a mobile storage unit during the opening. It was ironic that, when we held the launch of the restaurant, all the furniture that makes it what it is had to be moved off-site. Now Angela and her staff had the job of putting everything back in place, ready for breakfast service and the next stage in the 105 years of The Connaught's life.

The early days after the opening were full of comment. Here was a female chef taking on the Establishment and bringing to the restaurant-going public an address that no one ever really considered going to unless their father and grandfather had done so or they were a guest staying in the hotel. Not only that, but suddenly there was an attractive menu and volumes of seductive PR to draw people in. I always think that, when you open a restaurant, you get just one chance. The question in the mind of every guest on their first visit is simple: will I come back? On that, coupled with the food writers' columns, will depend the success of any new restaurant.

It was not plain sailing for a good reason. The reservations book was full for the first month, and the hotel guests had nowhere to go. The days of sallying forth from your room to a half-empty restaurant, where you would be shown to your usual table by one of the undertakers before being overpowered with done-to-death lamb chops, were over. Not only that, but the old brigade couldn't quite understand why reservations were spaced in quarters of an hour. Dinner is always at 8 p.m. and always has been, and now this woman tells me that I can only get a table at 8.45 p.m. How extraordinary! The letters of complaint piled in. A woman is in charge. My corner banquette seems to have disappeared. The lamb was pink, and there was a foreign waiter who couldn't understand what I was saying. Where has the dessert trolley gone? I'm sure the head waiter was just wearing an ordinary suit. All letters in our business are replied to the next day, if possible. A complaint is a complaint, and a soothing explanation may go some way to introducing this peeved guest to a new, lighter way of life. But, at the same time, the press were printing words of approval in their columns, and we started receiving letters of congratulations. More importantly, the reservations book remained full.

We had transferred about thirty staff members from the *ancien régime* to our newly opened restaurant. For every successful transfer, there is usually a disaster. The disaster comes first. In this case, the story ended in an industrial tribunal, and we had to pay out £30,000. The only silver lining was that we had learned how to conduct ourselves in court. On the other side of the coin, Angela spotted a young chef called Diego Cardoso, and knew at once that he had what it takes. In the dining room, you can hide incompetency and laziness, but not so in the kitchen. One by one, all of the transferred kitchen staff met their Waterloos and went the way of the sinking stove and the rat's nest. Diego stayed and, in time, became one of Angela's trusted lieutenants. When interesting weeks came up, it was Diego who was put forward to represent *The Connaught*, and within a year, he had travelled with me to Moscow and later opened *Cielo*, Angela's restaurant in Florida.

The Connaught is much smaller than Claridge's, ninety-odd rooms, compared to over 200. The hotel staff are much more in-your-face, and the integration between the two cultures is not smooth. We are running the staff canteen, and we feed each member of staff for £50 a month. This is the main area of contention, and, in desperation, we tore out the old staff kitchen – which, incidentally, was still run by the same brigade that ran it before we came along – and installed a new range. The complaints still kept coming in, and I realized that this was something that would never change. My only enjoyment was when we banned smoking in the restaurants, applying the same rule to the staff canteen.

I was standing outside on the pavement one day when a cab drew up, and inside I could see Gillian Thomson struggling with a pile of menus. She had come up from the office, and I saw that the member of the foyer staff on duty had slipped away. Gillian had to struggle with a fare to pay and a door to open, and it was raining stair rods. By the time I had helped her and gotten her inside, I was ready for this knobhead, and went to find him.

'Thanks for your help, big man,' I said.

He turned, and I saw that he was dressed immaculately. Polished shoes and straight tie. Not a team player, I thought.

He replied slowly. 'Listen, Ramsay, you keep your fucking nose in the kitchen, and I'll do my job as I see fit.'

All I could think was that this man would single-handedly close the hotel if he was allowed to stay. He didn't stay.

Unlike at *Claridge's*, we have a complex of revenue streams at *The Connaught*. There are two restaurants, the main dining room and the smaller grill room. There is the front bar, the American Bar, the Red Room, room service and two private dining rooms, including the Carlos Room. There is also revenue from the staff canteen. All these have to be recorded and scrutinized. Having this number of areas of responsibility also means more staff, sometimes located in areas of little revenue. The Red Room serves light breakfasts and lunches and, later, afternoon tea. It needs staff in attendance all the time, although, for many guests, it is a quiet area where they can sit and read for hours without spending the price of a canapé. The hotel still employs the original room service butlers who take the trays from the pantries, and we just charge for the food and beverage. All this has to be recorded and accounted for. When the time came and we saw that *The Connaught* was not a gushing fountain of cash, all these revenue streams had to be taken apart and examined. Two years passed before we finally had control, and we had learned a very important lesson. Detail in accounting tells everything, and I had our accounts staff strip out every factor that drained the money flow. From increasing the number of covers in the restaurants to checking the suppliers' invoices against the delivery notes, to locating every lost tablecloth and napkin and securing the stock controls, we gradually took control and the losses began to shrink. *Claridge's* had spoiled us, and we were now having to work hard to get our latest venture right. It was no fucking good making money up the road and pouring it down the drain 200 metres away, and that's what we were doing before things changed. But then, all of a sudden, everything was up in the air again.

Sometimes Blackstone's visions went too far. They had got it into their heads that an area immediately outside the hotel could be turned into a winter garden. They planned for a glass conservatory to be built against the grand, curving front elevation, and this was to be a beautiful informal café in the French style. It was doomed almost from the start, as work commenced even before the all-powerful planning committee of the City of Westminster had given its blessing. There clearly hadn't been enough kissing of the ring, and down the hoarding came. Months later, it went back up, and on to the front of this stunning building was clipped a greenhouse. No one had really worked it out, and there were walkways that went nowhere and there was no way to enter it from the hotel. For a few weeks, we tried to make it work, but it was a forlorn hope, and one day, someone came and took it away. Just like that. It had cost £600,000. What was interesting was how many people didn't notice its disappearance, and I was one of them.

By the time Blackstone sold the Savoy Group to the Irish Quinlan Private Equity Group, The Connaught needed some urgent attention. As Derek Quinlan once said, 'If a guest is paying £750 a night, he is entitled to a shower that works.' So, finally, The Connaught was to get some full attention. Blackstone had already worked out the difficult bit of how to add another thirty-two rooms, and had made models to prove it. No doubt they also had planning permission, which must have been a mission in itself with the City of Westminster, but within two years of the purchase, The Connaught was closed and undergoing a major renovation within an oxygen tent of scaffolding and polythene.

In the meantime, we were left with the decision of whether or not to go back when it partially reopened and face two years of brick dust, jackhammers and weak revenue streams, or to say goodbye and find Angela something different to do.

CHAPTER NINE

I WORE THE WHITES

*Organization is everything and should
never be ignored. Let only those who
can organize do so.*

ALMOST OVERNIGHT, WE had developed from a small restaurant in a Chelsea side street to the makings of a global brand. It happened so quickly, and we urgently needed an organization to deal with it. We had to learn some important lessons about how to build offices with the right people inside, because, without them, we had nothing but the prospect of chaos and we had to learn quickly.

In the early days, it never occurred to me that we should run our restaurant from *Royal Hospital Road*. It was a cramped area with little space outside the kitchen and the dining room, so, even from the beginning, we looked for a small office. Although, admittedly, this was an unwelcome overhead, I knew – even at that stage – that we would need somewhere to run the company and handle any business affairs that might come my way.

To begin with, Chris was operating from home. The bank proposal, the setting up of the company, insurance and letters of appointment all came from his dining room table, and he drove everyone mad. Business and homes just don't work in my book, and after these initial tasks, it was time to move to a different location.

We found a small office at 208 Fulham Road, almost opposite the Chelsea and Westminster Hospital. It needed painting and a new carpet, but it had high ceilings and was light and airy. Not a shoebox, but in later years, that is how we looked back at it. It was shaped like a letter 'E' without the middle bit, so Chris was hidden away at one end, and his secretary at the other end acted as a receptionist for all who walked through the door.

Good office practice was not only relatively simple with one restaurant, but was to become the bedrock of any future development. All the areas of management that would later become departments were, in those days, handled by the same person, who, of course, was Chris. It was then that the unwritten, unspoken work ethic developed between Chris and myself. Quite simply, I wore the whites, Chris wore the suits. But just as everyone was becoming aware that 'Ramsay' signified detail and a striving for perfection, the same imprint was to become stamped on the office.

I recall a late-night phone call from Jo Barnes, who had made the decision to leave Quadrille, our then publishers, as their press officer and start up Sauce Communications. This was the firm that became our PR machine. On this particular day, she had sent over two of her 'Saucettes' to prepare and post the invitations for the opening of *Pétrus*. Apparently, Frilly and Frothy had duly come over and clucked around all afternoon as they banged out the cards, stuffed them in envelopes and started to stick on stamps. Chris had wandered over and taken a handful from the pile. Having cast his eye over them, he called a halt to the proceedings and invited the two girls to sit down for a minute. They thought they were about to be congratulated on their speed and resourcefulness, and their mouths dropped when it was pointed out that, in a sample of ten cards, three names had been spelled incorrectly, there were fingerprints on the envelopes, and the stamps were stuck on like fridge magnets.

'Girls,' came the message, 'if you are going to do something, then do it fucking properly or go home and paint your nails.'

The cards went out without a wrong name, in immaculate envelopes and with stamps that lined up. This is not anal, nor is it obsessive–compulsive. It is just a matter of getting things right. It's as easy to stick the stamp straight as it is crooked. But how you do it tells the whole story. The recipient of the invitation doesn't look at the envelope and excuse the misspelled name, the thumb mark and the Queen looking askance because it was one of 500 envelopes. It will be taken personally. Why is mine like this? Don't I matter enough for someone to get it right?

One thing is for sure: Frilly and Frothy never got it wrong again, and the late-night phone call from Jo Barnes was to tell me that my office was being run like my kitchen.

With a payroll of only thirty-five and one set of books to look after, there was time to look at different proposals, to plan book launches and, of course, to look for another restaurant. *Pétrus* came along, and suddenly we were looking at an extra thirty on the payroll and two sites to keep our eye on.

Were we comfortable now, with plenty to keep us occupied and more money coming in than I could ever have imagined? I don't think the question ever arose. It all felt like the start of a long journey to me, and it was just a question of looking at the opportunities and deciding how we needed to arrange our limited resources to make the most of them.

What was interesting was that the office had now grown to include a full-time human resources manager, a bookkeeper and a maintenance man. We didn't quite need these full-time appointments, but it gave a plain signal to everyone that we were not standing still with two little restaurants, but looking hungrily around. When the *Gordon Ramsay at Claridge's* invitation came, we were in a position to respond. There was no fancy office to show anyone around and there wasn't much of a track record in terms of organization. But we could begin a list of what we needed to put together, and suddenly the office was fizzing with life.

HR had the immediate job of looking at all the transferees from Claridge's prior to the signing of the deal. We needed to know what the likely liability in taking over these employees would be, knowing that some of them had been around since Noah launched his cruise ship for couples. In the event, no one transferred, so HR had to redirect their efforts to interviewing and enrolling a whole new kitchen brigade and front-of-house team. At the same time, training programmes had to be devised and operated, and it was not long before the HR team had grown to three.

The logistics of *Gordon Ramsay at Claridge's* demanded that we compose endless lists of orders for all the usual tableware, including glasses, silverware, porcelain, tablecloths, cruets, uniforms, kitchen utensils, pots, pans and a thousand incidentals. Not only did we itemize what we required, but we then had to choose them. It was not just a question of what looked good but, much more importantly, what would look good in a year's time. Longevity meant money saved, and we looked hard at our intended purchases. If the porcelain plates bore a platinum line and looked beautiful, the plates would be put through the commercial dishwashers 200 times. When this brutal action revealed the wearing away of the line, then we knew that these products were for the domestic market. Just buy the plates without the platinum line, and they will still look beautiful and last until they meet their doom at the hands of a clumsy and soon-to-be-sacked commis waiter.

The concept of longevity is an element of common sense. Common sense was to serve us well, and to it, over the years, was added experience. It taught us how to think things through in a practical way. You didn't need a fortune-teller. You just needed to tread the intended path before going public. I think back to the decision to buy in antique silver tea and coffee pots. I knew that they would look great on the white tablecloths, and it wasn't easy to source so many at once. What made the task harder was that we had worked out that only pots with insulated handles could be used. There had to be a break between the pot and the grip area of the handle to ensure that the heat didn't make it impossible to hold. In most cases, these were fillets of ivory or ebony beautifully worked in so that no one would even notice. Just details, but so important.

I sometimes look at a beautiful building being opened with all the majesty of the State Opening of Parliament, only to see the place decline in its looks within a couple of years. In creating a design that will sit on the cover of *Architectural Digest*, the architect will have forgotten that if you design a building in the centre of a busy, dirty metropolis, someone will need access to clean it. Why should he care? The Queen cuts the opening tape, he collects his immense fee and moves on to the next project. Walk through London and see how many stone recesses collect filth or become homes for pigeons, and how rust drains down from metallic fixings until a building's façade screams of neglect. All because the days ahead had not been an issue for the designer. In ten years' time, the building will be swathed in scaffolding and bandages while a fortune is spent on bringing it back to life. Or, worse, it remains an eyesore.

In restaurants, the same rule applies. Look at the demands of maintenance and make them as easy as possible. Otherwise, they will be neglected. There is a well-known restaurant with a huge, beautiful canopy over the open kitchen. In all the years that I have seen this, it has never had less than an inch of dust covering it. It's out of reach of a weekly wipe, so everyone conveniently forgets about it. Everyone, that is, except the diner.

The study of a restaurant and the movements, sight-lines and habits of its guests all combine to give a clear indication of what needs to be planned early on. A restaurateur would do well to look at all aspects of the operation. Take the 'ladies and gents' as an example: you should play the role of the guest, listing a thousand considerations, all of which will take you a step towards getting it right. From a seat in the restaurant, your guest will want to navigate a route to the loo with as little fuss as possible. A well-trained waiter will gently indicate to you that he knows what's on your mind and lead the way. Nothing beats this for guest attention. The waiter is stopping everything to look after you in your moment of need. No questions necessary, and no need for the guest to wonder what word to use if they are feeling uncomfortable about the word 'lavatory'. Plan this into your training manual. If the establishment doesn't quite run to this level of anticipation, then the diner will be looking for clear, discreet signage. Design it and test it.

The doors leading to a lavatory in a restaurant are critical. Gentle swing-doors are to be considered. Who wants to touch handles in a place like this? This is Grand Central, where, in gastronomic and digestive terms, what goes in has to come out, and the two do not sit comfortably with each other. Use immaculate white basins and avoid modern, designer-inspired but impossible-to-understand taps that can't be controlled with soapy fingers and show no indication of hot and cold. The less you need to touch, the better. Bars of soap are totally out of the question. They have been used two minutes earlier by Sloppy Larry. Wet hands need a clean individual towel right next to the basin, not several steps away along a path of drips on the floor leading to the nearest roller towel or jet drycr. Make sure that there is plenty of mirror space on the wall – full-length mirror space. Returning to the dining room means being back on parade after a personal readjustment, and it can be a tad embarrassing when zips are still at half-mast, or a flimsy dress has somehow got caught up in your big pants.

Don't forget that most women don't have a pee holding their handbags. There has to be somewhere to put them, along with jackets. Loo doors without a decent, large hook are as infuriating as a lock that doesn't offer you full protection. I recall, when we opened in New York, how the designer locks were impossible to slide shut, often leading to a difficult encounter, no matter which side of the door you were on. Unfortunately for us, an important food critic was caught with his trousers around his ankles by his counterpart from a different newspaper. You could hear the laughter on Fifth Avenue, and a week later, when the critic filed his report, although the locks had been fixed, the horse had bolted and was halfway up Broadway. We got a seriously indifferent write-up, and I realized how much I curse careless problems.

Above all, make sure that these temples of relief are cleaned regularly, and I don't mean daily. Someone has to do it, and if it means checking every fifteen minutes, then make arrangements from Day One. Years ago, I was sitting in a busy restaurant with a starter of croque-monsieur when suddenly this French guy came out of the loo shouting at the head waiter about the disgusting sight he had just witnessed. This was a bit ironic, coming from a Frenchman, and I thought that he must have found a dead body or something. But it had the most appalling effect on everyone. They just got up and left. It was like the fire alarm had gone off.

So this is what we did in the office. We thought things through. The shoebox was straining to contain our growing energy, and it was clear within six months of opening *Gordon Ramsay at Claridge's* that we needed to look for bigger offices. We had taken on a small office in Berkeley Square to cope with our private dining sales, but what I didn't want was the fragmentation of control. What we needed was to bring everyone under one roof.

One night after service, I was driving through the streets of Victoria and passed a small office block with a letting sign outside. I gave Chris a call the following morning, and within a month, we were ready to move in on three of the six floors. There was something about these offices that suited us. They were not modern, but had undergone extensive refurbishment, and somehow the developers had introduced some warmth and a bit of character.

Now we could separate the different departments. On the first floor, human resources took up position to make themselves accessible to the waves of new staff that would come through in the coming years. Training had become a department in its own right, and was nestling on the same floor. Upstairs there was private dining, which had moved from Berkeley Square, and across, on the other side of the floor, sat accounts and the number crunchers. In his eyrie on the fifth floor was Chris with his boardroom.

By this time we had taken on The Connaught, and the need for this office base was never greater. But the biggest step forward was in our reservations system. Until now, both *Royal Hospital Road* and *Pétrus* had held their own reservations books, while *Gordon Ramsay at Claridge's* had six reservationists buried in a windowless, airless Black Hole of Calcutta in the depths of Claridge's. We had heard of a new Scandinavian restaurant-booking system called Logos, and, after numerous tests, we opted for this. As the first to buy in this system in the UK, we were probably driven by desperation for a workable alternative to the manual reservation. It allowed all calls for any of the restaurants to patch in to Victoria, with the caller blissfully unaware that the person answering was not holding a pencil as she thumbed through the pages of the reservations book.

What Logos brought us was the power of cross-selling. When a call came in for a reservation at *Royal Hospital*

Road and there was nothing available, the reservationist would simply offer *Pétrus* as an alternative. It meant that the sale was not lost, and we had found a solution to someone's booking need. The figures that the system threw up showing converted calls told me that our investment was sound. Added to that, as soon as a caller's name was tapped into the system, up would pop a potted history of earlier visits. 'Jan. 18th 2004 Chocolate cake on Grannie's eightieth. Two grandchildren, Elspeth and Holly.' So the reservationist had fodder for rapport, if required.

Today we take 3,500 calls each day for restaurant reservations. How many volumes of the old reservations books would they have filled?

The growth of the office, our headquarters, made us into a three-ring circus. The kitchen, the dining room and the office were the three inseparable elements of the business. None could run without the others. The one problem, however, was cost. Running an office payroll that was to grow to sixty, in addition to all the overheads, was a costly affair, and almost always there were research and development costs that promised a future income but, at present, required a budget. Each restaurant provided a contribution in direct proportion to its turnover. Gordon Ramsay Holdings was the equity owner of the restaurants, but, in effect, was also employed by each of them and relied on their income to make ends meet. In addition, it had income streams from a number of consultancies to provide external training, advice or just the right to use my name. Always there was a chase for income, and it was through this that Gordon Ramsay and Gordon Ramsay Holdings began to move independently. I was to become consumed in television and publishing, while Holdings represented the brand to an increasing number of takers.

The concept of a headquarters controlling the restaurants was one that worked well. It didn't stifle them, and we always paid homage to the individuality of each chef and menu, and to the guest appeal that ensured a loyal following. We had viewed other operations where the same menu appeared in different settings, almost word for word, and that was not for us. A Gordon Ramsay restaurant was to represent quality of ingredients, high service standards and value for money. They were the only traits that bound the group members together.

The one single factor that allowed us to open so many restaurants in a relatively short space of time was the amazing stable of kitchen talent that had come out of the *Aubergine* days. Good people who had worked for me then may have gone their separate ways, but when their time came, they returned and took up a position within the group. Names like Mark Askew, Stuart Gillies, Angela Hartnett, Mark Sargeant and Marcus Wareing had all come from my earlier life, and they were to play key roles in the growth of Gordon Ramsay Holdings. In return, and at the right time, they acquired a percentage of the business they headed, and this guaranteed their continued loyalty. Not only that, but they were given the freedom to promote their own names with books and television appearances.

The company is built on the loyalty of brilliant chefs. I may sometimes be difficult to work with, and I may occasionally appear stubborn or offhand, but the fact is that I have fantastic people working for me, and this is how we make the company work. That is the lesson of organization: hire the right people and leave them to organize.

I now had three restaurants in London, including *Gordon Ramsay at Claridge's*, and one in Dubai, and one big office that could organize D-Day, but with heavy monthly overheads to pay. It had been put together with future expansion in mind, and to pay for all this, I had to do two things – get on with the expansion and look more seriously at the wider media to see if I could have a part to play there.

CHAPTER TEN

A CHANGE OF DIRECTION

*Too much all at once can
block the loos.*

ROYAL HOSPITAL ROAD, *Pétrus, Gordon Ramsay at Claridge's* and, to a large extent, *The Connaught* were flying the standard for fine dining. Fine dining is what I did, and that seemed to be what people expected from me. But sometimes I wondered how long I could keep it up as, even in a town like London, there had to be a limit to the number of Gordon Ramsay fine dining establishments. In truth, I hardly ever ate rich food myself, having tasted and retasted 100 dishes every night for ten years in the heat of a kitchen under continuous pressure. Haute cuisine, if I may use that slightly up-your-arse phrase, can be wonderful, but it creates a strong desire for simple, great-tasting café food, like steak and kidney pie or fish and chips, and in an extraordinary sequence of events, so typical of my life, I was suddenly confronted with the possibility of opening a café.

In the front bay of The Berkeley, a Savoy Group hotel in Knightsbridge, was *Vong*, the restaurant belonging to Jean-

Georges Vongerichten. It had been there for the past five years, and the agreement must have come to an end. By then, the owner of the Savoy Group was Blackstone, and I knew that John Ceriale would be striking a deal with *Vong* for the next ten years. Clearly, the shit hit the fan in some way, because suddenly Ceriale was on the phone to Chris, asking if he was interested in doing something if *Vong* continued to say no to whatever it was they had said no to. Chris replied, in his usual flat drone of indifference, 'Are you kidding? You bet your sweet arse we'll be there.'

Chris always forgot to use the American word 'ass', just as when he gives the finger, he always sticks up the wrong one, realizes it, and pretends he's hailing a cab. Perhaps the single most impressive thing about John Ceriale, apart from his vision, is that he is not about getting a rent for a space. What is important to him is to find a tenant who will make the place work and blend in with the hotel in question. John buys to sell, and he knows the value of detail. A successful restaurant is worth so much more than a restaurant that just manages to pay the rent. Well, isn't that so obvious?

Five days after that initial call, Chris and Ceriale shake hands. That's all that matters because the deal is now ours. We are going to do a café. Fuck, fuck, fuck. The interior designer has been appointed, the design is nearly complete, and we shall be opening in less than three months. Even the name is already decided on by the designer, for Christ's sake, and it is to be called the *Boxwood Café*.

'How cool is that?' I think to myself.

It would be nice to think that all I had to do was write a menu and off we go. Steak and kidney pie, plaice and chips, croque-monsieur, and chocolate ice cream to follow. But that wasn't going to happen, because what we were going to do was launch a café by Gordon Ramsay, and, for once, it seemed as though we had broken our golden rule. We had a restaurant, a theme and a deal, but no chef. The chef is always the starting point in anything we do, and my only consolation is that every rule may occasionally get broken. Also, we had exactly the right person to hand in the person of Stuart Gillies, who was faffing around with a restaurant project involving the ex-Caprice Holdings' owners. I had known Stuart for years, and loved his energy and intensity. He was like a bouncing ball and as bald as a coot, like one of the inmates in *One Flew Over the Cuckoo's Nest*.

The following three months were manic. Yes, we did have to write the menu, but we also had to sit down and understand the concept that we were about to embark on. How exactly could we make the jump between *Royal Hospital Road* and a café and maintain all credibility? The best discipline was to sit down with Sauce Communications, our PR firm, and work out what we were going to tell the press. That way, we would have set our course, and all we would need was a following wind.

The designer was from the US West Coast, and was beginning to get on my nerves. She had done a good job in turning what was an awkward, two-level, open-plan area into the semblance of a casual dining restaurant, with plenty of light colours and the feeling that you were in a rather pleasant greenhouse. But she wouldn't then let go of the bone. Her attention homed in on the tabletop settings, the menu, the plants on the tables and the staff uniforms. I had no problem with her enthusiasm, but once a designer turns their attention to our territory, Blackstone will start to forward her invoices to us. And we are not good at fees on that scale. In any case, you never have potted plants on a dining table unless your guests are going to be happy seeing worms and caterpillars crawling across their rib-eye steaks. The waiters were to be dressed in a mixture of Tyrolean lederhosen and a gardener's pyjamas. Impractical, more expensive than the Pope's Easter Sunday outfit, and looking fucking ridiculous. I told the designer to back off a bit, which she did when Stuart did his impression of Uncle Fester from *The Addams Family*. That was all very well, but I had to tread carefully, as John Ceriale always laid his life down for those designers whom he kept pulling out of the hat. I remember his credo: a restaurant needs a location, a chef and a designer. Well, fine, but you don't have to go to their church, for Christ's sake.

While all this was going on, we were doing another deal with Blackstone down the road at The Savoy, and, in many ways, it was a 'step there if you dare' arrangement. I really wanted The Savoy. It had glamour and desperately needed change. It was sliding downhill at a rate of about 15 per cent a year, and Blackstone knew they were going to have to do something pretty damn quick. The only problem was that *The Savoy Grill* was making money, a great deal of money, and Ceriale said, quite candidly, that he couldn't give us that restaurant because we could never afford the rent. Any deal would have to be structured in such a way that it would give the owners the same profit they were currently enjoying, which left small pickings for anyone looking for a margin outside of that.

The success of *The Savoy Grill* all centred on lunch. It was bang in the centre of the City, so lunch was very busy, but there were no takers in the evening because everyone had gone home. *The Savoy Grill* at lunch was filled with power-broking bosses from every big corporation and the Establishment. Its patrons didn't look at the menu; they already knew it by heart. They were far too busy taking stock of whom their fellow diners were with and, more importantly, where they were sitting. In the evening, the restaurant would count itself lucky if it had thirty guests, and it was there that we could see a window of opportunity.

Chris met with Ceriale and Bill Stein, his numbers man. Fuck knows what they talked about and how they shuffled the numbers, but they all shook hands afterwards and Chris emerged from the meeting to say that *The Savoy Grill* was ours. Fucking hell. We're off again. As much as Chris adored Ceriale, he was always happy when Bill Stein was around. He was Mr Rational, and sometimes a visionary like John needs a bit of stabilizing, so the two made a real A-team. Luckily, they seemed to like us a lot.

The same designer who was working on *Boxwood* in The Berkeley was also given *The Savoy Grill* by Blackstone. This was a seriously difficult brief because we were back to the same story about not offending the existing clientele, which we had faced at *The Connaught*. I think the designer did an amazing job although she used exactly the same ceiling paper in both venues, which pissed off a few purists.

So, in *The Savoy Grill* we had nothing to lose in the evening, but at lunchtime, we had a sizeable income at stake, and it would be vital to keep the regular guests. The restaurant manager had been in charge for donkey's years, and considered himself to be pivotal to our success or failure. His first demand was for some suits, and we obliged. He was a pleasant enough man who had learned the trick of the constant smile to hide darker thoughts, and after only a few weeks, he promptly left to join the Forte heir in Dover Street, where *Brown's* was about to be clad in scaffolding for a two-year refurbishment. This was probably a case of crap timing, as far as our departing manager was concerned, because if the idea was to take our lunch clientele away with him, he would have to wait nearly two years before he had a restaurant to feed them in. My only sorrow at his departure was that we had paid for the fucking suits.

There was a great lesson here: if you are going to make a clean sweep, then do so. A fixation on retaining one person to continue what you are essentially trying to change doesn't make sense. He represents history, while you are busy constructing the future. For the price of two suits, learning that lesson was absolutely worth it.

Lunch service continued at a pace. The only real problem was that everyone arrived on the dot of one o'clock to be fed. That's what happens when you go to public school: a rigid timetable. We were used to spacing tables at gaps of a quarter of an hour, thereby giving the kitchen time to devote to each guest. What they had been used to was an indifferent menu, but one designed for plenty of pre-cooking and leaving the sausage toad or spotted dick in the bain-marie for quick service. It was a case of: never mind the taste, just get it there in time. You may be assured that our offerings were never going to go down that route. However, we did have to do some serious replanning of the dishes on offer to try and get them into the dining room, and I think we must have achieved a degree of success, because the lunch service started to increase.

The evening trade changed like you wouldn't believe. The old trolleys and Bunsen burners, so reminiscent of *The Connaught,* were thrown out, and in came a beautiful, light, modern menu to complement the now very elegant dining room. Everyone, it seemed, suddenly wanted to come to *The Savoy Grill* for dinner. Lunch, unbelievably, was taking second place. Turnover was shooting up, and it seemed like the risk was paying off. We had reconstructed the kitchen and installed as head chef Josh Emmett, a tall, good-looking New Zealander who controlled his kitchen brigade with a rod of iron. His attitude and energy were setting him on the path to prominence, and within four years he would be running New York and LA for the group.

And if that wasn't enough, we were also busy moving *Pétrus* from its original site in St James's Street into The Berkeley, replacing my old mentor Pierre Koffmann's *La Tante Claire*. How weird is that? He had brought *La Tante Claire* from Royal Hospital Road to The Berkeley, and now I was again taking over Pierre's vacant restaurant site. Blackstone had brought in David Collins to design the new *Pétrus*, which concerned me, as I had never been a fan of the Collins Museum of Modern Design. Ironically, his first restaurant ever had been *La Tante Claire* some fifteen years earlier. It was very stylized and perfect at the time, but everything I had seen since looked as though it was destined for the business-class lounge at Manchester Airport. The brief for *Pétrus* could be summed up as 'the view from inside a bottle of Bordeaux'. When the roughs, the visuals and, finally, the finished restaurant were presented, I realized we had one of the most beautiful restaurants in London. Red, velvet, modern and as chic as a Paris catwalk. All we had to do was launch the new *Pétrus* and look forward to the second Michelin star by the beginning of the new year.

With its fabulous dining room, discreet private dining area and Chef's Table overlooking an immaculate, slick kitchen, *Pétrus* did extremely well from the beginning. It was a much easier act than its previous address at 33 St James's Street. There were no stairs between the kitchen and the dining room, for a start, and it was properly equipped with new Rorgue stoves and everything else that a chef would die for. Strangely enough, Marcus Wareing decided to take it 'private' and rebuffed any offers of help. It was the first time that I had not been asked to any tastings and for advice. I could understand that Marcus was trying to create his own imprint, but it's a brave man who doesn't turn to his fellow chefs for some free advice. The unsurprising result was that, in spite of Marcus's undoubted talent, the reviewers didn't go overboard with *Pétrus*. They loved the dining room, but found the complexity of flavours on the plate overpowering. He had also done some pretty daft things, such as using long, intricate descriptions for each dish on the menu and changing the appearance of the menu, with brown type on a saffron-coloured background with a Palace Script font. It looked naff, and was impossible to read in the dimmed light of the restaurant. It was also the complete opposite of our Century Schoolbook 14-point black-on-white standard menu, which a blind elephant could read along the length of his trunk. It pointed to the fact that Marcus wanted to be different, to highlight his own professional identity, but, in doing so, he perhaps showed more clearly the need for the guiding hand of Gordon Ramsay Holdings. The menus were rewritten and reprinted, but, even, so it would be another three years before Michelin bestowed a second star on *Pétrus*.

The effect on Gordon Ramsay Holdings and, in particular, Gillian Thomson, with three openings almost at once, was pretty shattering. We had simply taken on too fucking much, and it became vital that this growing chaos did not spill out on to the dining room floors. We split the operations into squads to deal with all the problems of this overcrowded maternity clinic, where all the babies had popped out at the same time, and gradually some order was restored. In fact, we got away with bloody murder.

Pétrus and *The Savoy Grill* made money from Day One. *Boxwood*, on the other hand, did not. It would be at least a year before that began to happen, in spite of the gallant efforts of Stuart and his team. This had been a change in direction for the group, and it was our first try at showing that we could do something else. The restaurant journalists liked it in principle, but wanted to make a big thing about whether it was a café or not. What's a café? It had been called 'café' because that distinguished it from a fine dining restaurant, but, of course, it still had some of the fine dining features, such as silver, white linen and a slightly formal service. What did they expect? A floozie waitress with a fag hanging from her mouth and a chef with fat all over his front?

In time, and with Stuart's persistence, a loyal clientele began to emerge, and soon it became known as London's best-kept secret. I'm not sure that was so clever at first, but now word has gotten out, and *Boxwood* is generally loved by all. More importantly, it is making good money.

We had still one more adventure in London with Blackstone.

There is a hotel on the north-east corner of Grosvenor Square. It's a Marriott operation, and it got scooped up by Blackstone from its Japanese owners, apparently for a song, but I don't know who was singing. John Ceriale called Chris and explained that he had it in mind to bring Joël Robuchon's new *L'Atelier* operation from Paris into the restaurant, which fronts Grosvenor Square. You cannot see the hotel entrance from the square, and there is a flight of steps leading up to the restaurant, making it appear as if it's a standalone site. John wanted Chris to help Joël's team set up the restaurant, and, to be quite honest, we had no problem with that. So a meeting was set up between Joël Robuchon, his Greek partner and their team to liaise with Chris, who had put together some information on the joys of running a restaurant in London. After that meeting, we never heard another word from them until John came back on the scene and said that, following a row, disagreement or impasse, he had told them to fuck off. Interesting in itself, but not nearly as interesting as when John asked if we could put something similar there ourselves.

Jason Atherton had taken over as our executive chef in Dubai after Angela had left to come and run *The Connaught*. He had now completed his two-year tour, his golf handicap had improved immeasurably, and it was time to come back to us and take on something a bit more demanding. What better than this new Mayfair opportunity? Jason is a great chef. He has worked in the most unlikely places, including *El Bulli* in Spain, under Ferran

Adria, and was perhaps the most open, committed and talented cook I had come across. The moment we started to talk about this new site, he sat up, and from then on, he was pushing forward to make it the most successful restaurant in London. While John Ceriale played around with designers, we started mapping out a fresh concept, avoiding fine dining, but looking at the finest ingredients. This was to be a menu of French tapas with an oriental influence, and suddenly Jason was coming up with some intense, dynamic flavours that made me think we were on to a winner here.

The name was to be *maze*, a concept that came from the New York designer and which seemed to catch the imagination. The kitchen was planned in a line, rather than the usual island layout, so that as guests walked through, they could see the whole operation at work. It looked awesome, and, as ever, we had a Chef's Table and private dining room, both right in the eye of the storm.

maze opened and became an immediate hit. It had a long bar at the entrance that led into a series of open rooms, so that on each visit you could imagine that you were at a different restaurant. It looked like, um, a maze.

Blackstone was very proud of this restaurant, which had just fallen into our lap, thanks to Joël Robuchon. However, they didn't get sentimental over it, and within a year, they sold the hotel to Strategic Hotels. The new owners took a while to get their feet under the table, but suddenly they were our new friends and, realizing the effect that the restaurant was having on the hotel's business, they asked if we would consider opening a further part of *maze* and taking over the whole food and beverage operation in the hotel. At the time of writing, we are just on the point of signing the deal, which will bring in a new concept restaurant called *maze Grill*, opening in the spring of 2008.

maze had shown that we could do something very different and do it well. It is, without doubt, a concept that is easily transportable. It has already taken over the more relaxed part of *Gordon Ramsay* in New York, and is scheduled for one or two other exotic locations.

CHAPTER ELEVEN

FOR SALE: INTELLECTUAL PROPERTY

Building a brand has unlimited value. It might not appear on a balance sheet, but it has a name that everyone wants.

So THERE WE were with our successful group of restaurants, with a big office infrastructure and the new operation at *The Connaught* still costing us money. We knew that new revenue streams would pick up as we expanded, but we needed them now to finance our research and development into new projects. The answer lay in two pompous-sounding words: 'intellectual property'. And I was going to have to learn exactly what they meant.

School, with its mission to teach little brains how to become bigger brains, somehow passed me by. I have always had a pressing need to not concentrate for very long, and my arse needs to move when it hears the sound of the human voice in the 'Are you paying attention?' mode. The term 'intellectual property', therefore, would be as unlikely a consideration in my life as advanced gynaecology would be in the simple existence of a Trappist monk. Well, I would have thought this to be the case until, of course, someone explained to me what IP actually meant.

I suppose the easiest way to understand, from a chef's point of view, what possible value these two little letters might have is to look at his recipes. It's not easy to make a recipe your own. Coca-Cola managed it, but still had to keep the recipe under lock and key in case some little toerag started to brew it in his bedroom at half the price. In the early days at *Aubergine*, I would put frothy concoctions on my menu that sold well and, to an extent, became my signature dishes. Visiting chefs love to roll into a successful restaurant on the pretext of tasting, when all they really want to do is to get up nice and close and work out how they can put froth all over their own little menus. And do they write on the menu, 'Courtesy of Gordon Ramsay'? Do they fuck. And yet this, I would argue in a very loud way, is my intellectual property.

The start of my IP earnings was in the publication of little booklets on pasta sauces. From memory, I think I got a fat cheque for £500 and blew it on a weekend in Paris. I am sure the booklets were a thrill for me at the time – you know, name in print and all that old fanny – but years later, the very same little works of erudition turned up in a super-market pack with a cheap white bowl and a bag of multi-coloured pasta. The packaging was no more than an acetate box with no printing on it. It didn't need any because, there inside, visible through the plastic box, was my huge, money-spinning booklet that said 'Gordon Ramsay'. Maybe I signed some obscure clause in the original contract that allowed them to do this. I can't now remember, but this was a welcome wake-up call to the world of intellectual property and its protection.

As real books started to emerge, so did advances and royalties. The first two books were my pride and joy, and could have consigned my publishing endeavours to some back alley of haute cuisine never to be heard of again. They were beautiful to look at, but were fledglings when it came to earnings. They were cooks' cookbooks, and in those naïve days, it never occurred to me that, by specializing like this, I was limiting the market or, to put it in easy-to-understand terms, screwing myself with vanity. I mean, what is the use of publishing a book on extreme cuisine when the average cookbook-buyer wants to know how to make a delicious croque-monsieur or tarte Tatin?

The publishing house that I was tied to must have just had a lobotomy or something because, as the second book came out, they decided that it didn't need any launch or marketing. If the truth were known, it was probably more to do with a slight reputation I seemed to be acquiring as a good chef who spoiled the show with naughty swear words, usually starting with 'f'. How fucking ridiculous was that? And it was a caution that spread through all the money-making opportunities that I had hoped would make me Ferrari-rich. The television broadcasters just averted their eyes like my flies were wide open.

But, as so often happens, someone looked sideways, and before I knew it, a new publisher was on the scene. Quadrille Publishing came along with a push from my then agent. It was probably the only time these agents did anything of real significance for me, and by the time Chris arrived and sacked them, we were looking to publish *A Chef for All Seasons*. It also marked the start of my intense dislike for agents, whether they are estate, literary, talent or, my own personal favourite, recruitment vultures, whose appetite for commission far outstrips their inclination to do any work. Lazy arseholes.

A Chef for All Seasons was to be the first real cookbook that turned me into a writer of real food books that could be used in a kitchen near you. Quadrille knew about the mix of photography, clearly written step-by-step recipes and a marketing drive through all the major bookselling cities in the UK. The book sold brilliantly, and I began to make some money.

As I had mentioned earlier, the television broadcasters were very wary of the effect that I might have on their already dwindling kitchen audiences. Cookery had gone through its golden age of Fanny Cradock in the sixties, and, in recent years, the *Ready Steady Cook* recipe was looking very tired. Certainly no one saw me as the answer to securing 10 million viewers.

But from one programme-maker came the idea of a camera following me around during the working day. 'Fly on the wall', I believe, was the phrase they seduced me with, and, as always in those days, there was little or no money involved. *Boiling Point* was to be screened just as I was opening *Gordon Ramsay* in Royal Hospital Road with Chris. Poor guy. He had invested heavily in this restaurant, and, just as we opened, he would have to sit at home on Thursday evenings watching these programmes, in the certainty that, the following day, there would be mass cancellations of reservations. The truth is that it did us no harm. Far from it, but I still knew that TV screens were not quite ready for me, and that the time was not yet right.

Interestingly, the first real approach came four years later, when ITV asked me to appear in a new type of show they were doing, to be called *I'm A Celebrity ... Get Me Out Of Here!* This would have meant three weeks of filming in Australia, and I was definitely up for it. Chris wasn't, and said so. I sulked.

This stalemate would have continued until Chris, little bastard, played his trump card and pointed out that, for three weeks, I wouldn't have a mobile. I can't live without a phone for more than ten minutes, so that was that. In retrospect, when I see what total, utter crap that programme became, I grudgingly agree that my non-appearance was one of the better things that happened in my life. I guess I was just flattered by this sudden TV interest in me, and it would have been cool to be in front of 10 million viewers. Up to then, I would have been happy with an appearance on *The Sky at Night*.

The IP business also took a bite out of my backside when I got a bit cocky during a cooking demonstration using Bramley apples, which was being filmed on *Boiling Point*. I stood in front of these ladies who lunch, flashing my pans, cooking up a tarte Tatin or something, when the whole bloody pan goes up in flames. So I'm there, trying to rescue the show, having some fun, and I got a little carried away and, rather mischievously, switched from Bramleys to Granny Smiths, and referred to the then chairman of the Bramley Apple Campaign Group as a plonker. Talk about biting the hand that fed you. Two weeks later, about forty Bramley apple protesters appeared outside *Royal Hospital Road*, right in the middle of lunch service, with placards and county wellies. They had probably come down on tractors and a combine harvester. In the end, I had to return the £3,500 fee with a red-faced apology. They, unlike me, already knew about the protection of their intellectual property.

In the early days after *Royal Hospital Road* and *Pétrus* had opened, and while my book publishing was still wrapped in a cookery narcissism, the main IP ventures were directed towards product endorsement. Now, this is a very difficult area. We were not having to knock on doors, hoping that different brands might be persuaded to adopt me as their iconic guru, but, rather, we were flooded with people coming to us with propositions. The problem was, of course, that they never had any money and were looking to me as a strategy of last resort – a man who might just save their backsides from the friction burns as they slid down the helter-skelter of commercial failure.

One of the first punters was a beefy ex-chef who looked and behaved as though he had been pushing a barrow around Petticoat Lane for most of his sad life. He spread before me a million designs of chefs' jackets and a spread-sheet of projections that would have propelled him into the vaults of the Bank of England and given me a royalty suffi-cient to produce a gentle fart from my pottery piggy bank, which was standing empty on the kitchen table. He had all the credentials of a total failure, being a slob and an ex-chef, but he could talk the talk, and before we knew it, there were sample jackets coming in from Italy, or wherever 'his' factory was, for our chefs to try. All fucking exciting until two things happened. The first was that, during service, the jackets began to go yellow and the seams started to split. The second was that the fat ex-chef mentioned, sotto voce, that all he needed from me was £100,000 to launch the product. Goodbye, fat ex-chef. When my kitchen raised a collective eyebrow, as if to say, 'How could I be so fucking gullible?' I just looked at them and whispered, 'Chris's big idea,' so I escaped that particular humiliation. Chris was fine about it. Well, actually, Chris never knew what I said, so that was all right.

Then along came the great financial fiasco of the late nineties. The dot-com boom was not to make us rich, but we weren't to know that at the outset. A couple of Bright Young Things, who had CVs with names like Yale and

McKinsey sprinkled all through, asked us to become contributors to some recipe dot-com. All I had to do was lend my name as the standard-bearer and provide 1,000 recipes. Pages of sophisticated agreements arrived onto Chris's desk, and off we went, with recipes flying around and a continuous feed of how this particular dot-com would make all involved very rich people.

We had signed, and I think that we had even secured a £20,000 signature fee, when Chris went out to lunch with them. He came back and said two things. First, he could not believe that they had all chosen the most expensive dish on the menu, lobster or whatever, bearing in mind that this was a start-up, brand-new endeavour, and second, no one could quite explain where the revenue streams were to come from. I mean, open a restaurant, supply food and drink, and you present a bill. Easy stuff. But it suddenly became clear that these knobheads, with all their financial theory and scholarship, had convinced the investors to provide shedloads of seed money, ate lobster for lunch every day, and had yet to work out how the company's fucking income was to be charged.

Two months later, we were advised that the website was to be suspended, pending a redesign of the recipe pages, and I immediately realized that the dot in dot-com signified the end of the story. I never heard again from the two founding fathers, who, no doubt, had to skip the lobster for lunch from that day until they came up with their next Big Idea. Fortunately, Chris had retained the rights to the 1,000 recipes, and they would percolate through my books in the coming years.

Similar financial stillbirths happened a few times in these early days, as we concentrated most of our attention on the two restaurants. It wasn't so much that we lost money on these ideas, but, rather, we missed the opportunity to make the money, and gradually we learned how to say no. The restaurant business was about to take off, and perhaps, from that point of view, it was a blessing that we weren't sidetracked. It would all happen in time, but at this stage, we were trying to achieve too much and wasting a load of time. What we also learned was to look not only at a concept and the eventual agreement, but at the people involved. Look deep into their eyes and see if they are on a flight of fancy, or whether they have some idea of what they are talking about. Later we learned to look even harder at management structures, and decide whether people could do what they said they would do or whether we would be forever checking, prodding and pushing them to perform.

A Chef for All Seasons had really kick-started our book revenues, and I began to share Quadrille's enthusiasm and belief that books could be worth all the sweat and effort involved. Cookery books are like brain surgery handbooks. They have to be precise, clear and very accurate. A wrong measurement here or there and the soufflé doesn't rise and the brain drains. A cookery book has to be planned clinically, and the readership needs to be identified. Or, rather, you look for a million devotees desperate for some guidance in putting together desserts, boulangerie or 1,000 ways to cook an egg. The average cookery book will have over 100 recipes. These all have to be written and proofed, that is, the dish has to be produced in a kitchen, following the written instructions to the letter. There is also the photography, which means cooking the dish probably three times so that each critical stage can be photographed. Five recipes can take a whole day of photography, and most dishes have to be photographed. Get the text wrong, and you or your publisher will have a string of complaints for endless months after publication.

Book publishers are incredibly kind when it comes to putting money on the table. I don't necessarily say that they are overgenerous in the amounts that they pay, but there is this amazing formula whereby they pay up front their idea of how much the book is going to make in royalties. You sign the deal and you get a whack of money. You deliver the manuscript and, hey!, another splodge of dough, and later, just as the book goes on sale, even more pennies. Six months after publication, if the book has earned its advance, another big fat cheque arrives, and the whole venture has made everyone money.

So, we carried along in this direction with *Secrets*, followed by *Just Desserts*, and then *Gordon Ramsay Makes it Easy*. Each book not only earned its advance, but continued until it had done so two or three times over.

The *F Word* series on Channel 4 provided me with the first real opportunity to produce a book to go with a television show. We had done it once before, but under the control of the programme-maker, so the title went to a different publisher who, I felt, paid little attention to our thoughts. I remember the book as being indifferent, and although it sold reasonably well, those publishers would never see or hear from me again.

The *F Word* book was the time to look for a different publisher, in my mind. Quadrille had been brilliant, but I knew there was a bigger market out there. We needed a publishing house that could look after our overseas interests and knew the importance of an initial spend on marketing to propel foodies into the bookshops or, as is so often the case nowadays, the supermarkets.

I spoke about this with Chris, who had always been loyal to Quadrille, and, to an extent, he saw my point. He did, however, say that now was not the time. Firstly, there was a very limited time frame to produce *Sunday Lunch*, and there was simply not enough time to learn to work with a new crew. Secondly, it was unlikely that this TV book would achieve foreign sales. He was right, but I could see that he had taken my comments on board, so we stayed with Quadrille for this publication. And it has to be said that not only did they produce a great book in weeks, but they stepped up a whole quantum leap in the royalty leagues and the book achieved dizzying sales.

Looking back, I think that Quadrille mirrored the situation that happened with a number of people who worked with us. They just grew with us and managed to accelerate some of their ideas. Quadrille used to really piss me off because I saw them as penny-pinchers. I learned later that this is an understandable trait, as they never really know if the advance is going to be earned. But for me, as arrogant as a chef or an operatic diva can be, there was never the question of failure, and if I wanted more spent on marketing or first-class travel to book signings, then that is what had to happen. Gradually they learned this, but, by then, I had my sights on a bigger, global publishing house.

Poor Chris. He was being chased hard by ITV, who would not be deterred by my refusal to go for *I'm A Celebrity ... Get Me Out Of Here!* I remember sitting in on a meeting with some of their top executives, who were presenting him with the many reasons for joining, and he suddenly pitched up with the memorable, toe-curling statement that, in his view, ITV was like Tesco and Channel 4 was more akin to Waitrose. I don't think any of us really understood what he was trying to say, but you could have heard a fly poo on the carpet. Jo from Sauce Communications suddenly found the view across the rooftops irresistible, and I found my left shoe pretty interesting. The silence seemed to go on for ever until the meeting was called to an abrupt end. After everyone had gone, we turned to the soothsayer for his explanation. He was totally unaware that he had said anything of any significance, and suggested that we wait awhile and see if their offer was upped.

It was, of course, and suddenly we had committed ourselves to the production of something called *Hell's*

Kitchen for lots of money and a shedload of risk. It might be thought that *Hell's Kitchen* was a flop because I only did one series, but, from my own perspective, it was a triumph – more for what it led to than how it stood in the rankings of current entertainment.

Hell's Kitchen was experimental. It committed ITV to a very big spend, and no one quite knew how it would spin out. In the end, it worked, and ITV became hungrier for my talent. Fucking hell! Just listen to me. But it's true. When you hit the TV ratings, you become wonderful, amazing and marketable to the broadcaster, who thinks that it has just found the latest new talent who will bring the audiences, who will bring the advertisers.

So, Chris was being hounded by ITV executives, desperate to sign me up for the next three years. They really wanted me, and tried every trick in the book to secure my signature. A new contract would extend *Hell's Kitchen* to the United States, where Granada US could sell it to Fox. It would also hit Australia. I say that they tried every trick, but they missed one. While they were mapping out this amazing opportunity with all the options and opportunities to earn fees, Channel 4 suddenly appeared with a single offer of three-year exclusivity and my first-ever seven-figure cheque. On top of that, I would get paid for each episode of whatever programme we put together. And before I knew it, Granada US came along and we signed for *Hell's Kitchen USA* for the following five years as well.

ITV were pretty pissed off with Chris, but they were simply beaten to the line by a rival who, rightly or wrongly, worked out what they thought I was worth to them and made a bid. Eighteen months later, after I had just completed filming the second series of *Hell's Kitchen USA* in February 2006, ITV got all excited again and made a new offer to swing me back once my current contract with Channel 4 expired in 2007. Again, it was Chris who had to take the pressure. When they discovered he liked watching *A Touch of Frost,* they sent over a set of DVDs of every episode. Chris muttered something about not being corruptible, but I don't think that he sent them back. This is all very flattering but, fuck me, exactly the same thing happened again. While they were going into a million details of this new contract, Channel 4 waltzed in with a huge five-year offer, and that was that.

Understanding the power of your brand or image, or whatever, is not easy at the time. I don't think it's natural modesty that prevents me from realizing this strength. I guess that it just all happened so quickly. Gordon Ramsay Holdings had to look for a larger firm of accountants to represent us recently, and before I knew it, one of the big four firms was on our doorstep with a quote for auditing our accounts. I spoke to Sheldon Cordell from our lawyers, Joelson Wilson & Co., and he said that he wasn't a bit surprised.

'It's not the size of your account that they are after, Gordon,' he said. 'It's your name they want. It's a trophy.'

Right on. I have no problem with that if it helps get things done, but we didn't go with them anyway.

My intellectual property earnings started before I ever owned a restaurant. They were no more than fees for a recipe, an appearance, doing a demo and then a couple of books. The money went in my pocket and I didn't get too excited about it. When we started the restaurants, inevitably the earnings went into the company and helped our growth. But as they became more significant, I started to draw them out separately. Contracts were signed and the cheques came to me. So, almost overnight, we had the core business doing very well and we had what became described as my IP earnings. Sometimes they had to be divided. If staff like Jean-Baptiste Requien helped in *The F Word*, or I had a brigade of our chefs behind the pass helping a TV show, then this would count as a contribution by the company that would be paid by me.

Gordon Ramsay Holdings and its associated companies form what Chris still considers to be a small-to-medium-sized firm. It is also a family firm and unlikely ever to go public. However, there may come a time when we think about de-risking, selling off a minority shareholding to raise capital. Thinking about this makes me wonder what the company is worth, and I see at once an interesting aspect regarding the value. At present, Gordon Ramsay Holdings has revenue coming in from the restaurants, from a number of consultancies, and from a certain amount of endorsements. The numbers are very easy to work through, and it is not difficult to calculate our worth by looking at the profit and multiplying it by whatever number seems realistic. The problem is that there is no excitement like an oil well or gold mine that might suddenly take the firm into a different level of profits. Unless, of course, I were to include my intellectual property rights, which immediately bring an added value that doesn't require the use of the company's resources and an income that tends to be all profit. How clever is that?

CHAPTER TWELVE

AN INSPECTOR CALLS

*Protect yourself and always have
someone to count the
chocolate buttons.*

THIS IS A STORY about life. A life within a life, because not
only does it have a beginning, a fucking long middle and an
end, but it is upholstered with every imaginable emotion.
Looking back, it was one big bollock-kicking roller-coaster,
diving into the depths of despair and sailing straight up to
the heights and finding silver-edged clouds in the middle of
the worst possible fuck-up.

No Michelin inspector called here. No police or Special
Branch knocking heavily on my door in the middle of the
night. Far, far worse than that. Just an innocuous letter
asking for an appointment with Special Compliance Office
Leeds. It was addressed to me. To my home. It started: 'I am
writing to advise you that I intend making enquiries into
your personal tax returns under the discovery provisions of
Section 29 TMA 1970 for the 2001 Return and under
Section 9A TMA 1970 for the 2002, 2003 and 2004
Returns. The enquiries will be conducted under Code of
Practice 8 and I enclose a copy of that booklet for your

perusal. Please read it carefully.' Normally, this would have meant jackshit to me, to be perfectly honest, but Chris had been copied in, and when I saw him, I thought he had contracted a dose of epilepsy. It was like he had just entered his office and there, in the middle of the room, was a brown package with string, a collage of stamps and a sticker saying 'Unexploded Bomb'.

You go through life and you hear of, laugh at and immediately dismiss the taxman as a common hoodie out to harass you regarding your offshore accounts and bulging mattress. You feel safe, as this will never happen to you. But believe me, as I sit here as Gordon James Ramsay, a letter like this is the beginning of the purging of your financial soul. It is the start of a journey through space, where indignation changes into affront, to outrage, to screaming blue murder. And that's only the first interview. They should have government grants for counselling the poor fuckers who have had to deal with this letter. It's an affront to human rights, but, for once, such issues escape the gaze of liberals who are simply too tied up with paying their taxes and examining their carbon footprints.

When you're on the road most of the year, working your bollocks off to make things happen, keeping your head above water and sticking to the rules, you never expect anyone to think you are cooking the books. I know that our head office has everything counted, documented and filed, but I also know that my own financial life in the early days might not have been so. It never seemed like that at the time because money comes in and you need it. It gets spent and you think no more of it.

Chris said that he would handle this bombshell and I retreated, but for some reason, there were sharp needles injecting unease into my soft, tender parts. For the next few weeks, I sat on the sidelines watching, listening to and smelling fear. The meeting was arranged and the armourer's gaze fell on blunt, quiet instruments – ones that would tickle, compared to the sharp, red-hot poker that might later be required if the information dried up during the forthcoming enquiry.

On 7 April 2005, two men arrived at 1 Catherine Place. They were from Leeds and looked like it – grey, drab, anonymous and so polite you could scream before the provocation even began. Chris was brooding. This was like a visit to a dentist who is fresh out of anaesthetic. It hurt so much that it took me past ever being frightened again. But why was I scared? What was there to put the shits up me? No secret offshore bank accounts and no stacks of readies. Maybe just the odd petty cash backlog that we bypassed, rather than peeling apart a million taxi receipts, chewing gum wrappers and petrol bills.

We were presented with visiting cards showing that we were about to be entertained by Mr Delve and Mr Sifter, the gentlemen now sitting down at the boardroom table. Still so polite that it was cloying.

'Please tell us if, at any stage, you consider us impolite or rude.'

Fuck me! It seemed as though either of those charges, quietly suggested, might guarantee me a fast track to Belmarsh.

'Would you like some water?' I asked. 'Still or sparkling?'

The script, straight out of the dining room, was met with a request for tap water. Christ! Don't these turnips know that we run restaurants where Evian and Badoit pour like a mountain stream, compared to fluoridated, flat tap water? All the doors to the boardroom were closed. PAs had been given the afternoon off. Chris fetched a jug of tap water with a smile as watery as the waiter who knows that the only tip he'll be getting is the three o'clock at Kempton Park.

Mr Delve was the junior interrogator, and Mr Sifter sat quietly, legs apart, taking the occasional note. The former asked if I was familiar with the work of SCO. I replied that I wasn't, and felt like asking him if he was familiar with the difference between blue- and yellowfin tuna. He went on to say that SCO was a head office unit with a wide-ranging investigative role, generally involved with cases where there were avoidance aspects or serious fraud, or simply where there were substantial amounts of tax potentially at risk. Apparently, this enquiry was being conducted under Code of Practice 8, and there was no allegation of serious fraud at this stage. I noted the 'at this stage'.

Just so I would know where I was, Delve confirmed that there were 'a good number of issues to be covered' and that I might like to draw up a report addressing all the points. That way, he concluded, time and money would be saved in the long run, and we could cut out a good deal of correspondence. And so starts an interminably long line of tedious fucking questions. Shares that were disposed of years ago as part of a negotiated settlement and that were worth pennies should now apparently have had a huge value that I didn't declare. How did I pay for my house? 'It is understood, Mr Ramsay, that a significant amount was spent on refurbishments, and although you now earn a good salary, we have concerns over your overall means position. Delve tells me that £1 million has been mentioned.'

Chris countered by asking for their source, and Delve replied, like a Chinese mandarin, that the Revenue had a number of information sources available to it.

They moved on to the first flat that Tana and I owned in Battersea: how was it acquired, how much did it cost, and how was the cost met? They wanted to know what purpose the flat was put to while in my ownership, and what happened to the sale proceeds. Soon their questions fanned out to cover everywhere that I had lived since 1995. The same questions each time: where did the money come from? Who lived there? What were the dates of sale and acquisition? Did I buy the property for a relative?

Cars, my admitted weakness, now took centre stage. I had to go back and chart the history of cars in the life of Ramsay. Registration index, colour, price paid, all vehicles privately owned by myself or my wife. Delve couldn't resist his own summary, which included a Ferrari Marinello, a Range Rover, a BMW M3 and a Bentley. He said this just in case I claimed that I had only ever driven a Morris 1000. He wanted me to know that he knew all about me, and he was beginning to get my fucking goat. Half an hour had passed, and my arse was down to the bone.

We then moved sideways, and Sifter said that he was sure that Mr Ramsay would be aware of the interest that his colleagues in SCO Manchester had in the catering industry, which made the headlines some time ago. Fuck knows what he's talking about. He said they were looking at payments made to individuals by suppliers, and that this was an on-going project. Sifter then invited me to state if I had a dec-laration that I might wish to make about monies received from suppliers at any time. If there was, then he would like me to make it straight away. Was this man for real? Chris was immediately on his high horse because he knows how I feel about kickbacks or backhanders. He told Sifter in no uncertain terms that I, and, for that matter, he as well, saw the practice in the same light as drugs in the kitchen: it did not happen.

The meeting dragged on, and I was asked about employ-ing my sister as a nanny, and was it true that I received between six and twelve parking tickets a week? I then got the full force of SCO's intelligence-gathering. It started like heavy drops of rain just before the heavens open and it pisses all over you. We were back to Delve, who said they would like to look in some detail at my other income over the past six years or, as he put it, 'income over and above that shown on P60/P14'. I sat back as he recited all his homework. He went through my television shows, with dates, and then he spun out the titles of the books that I had published. I don't know where that information came from, but it was easily available. And then he paused and sucked his teeth.

'You had a 2005 calendar in the shops.'

He was referring to a one-off cookery calendar that netted me a massive, totally declared, above-board £10,000.

'Can you let me have a copy of the agreement, any royalty statements and a clear indication of where the proceeds were banked.'

I muttered under my breath, 'The Cayman Islands,' and for that, I got one of those sharp, under-the-table kicks from Chris. He wanted me to behave. I didn't want to. I wanted to tell those busy arseholes to go away.

They moved forward with headings like 'Your chocolate income,' 'A TV advertisement involving Walkers crisps from July 2004' and 'Your consultancy with Singapore Airlines'. Did I use them for my flights to the Middle East? Could I list my interview fees, as they were aware that I had done work for the BBC and Granada TV? Sifter came back to life and mentioned that he knew that I received £3,500 from Bramley apples some time before. Chris smiled sweetly, and said that it was true and that it was also true that Mr Ramsay had to repay the fee after insulting the chairman.

Sifter simply said, 'In that case, we shall move on to the lawsuit brought against you in America by one of the participants of *Hell's Kitchen USA*.'

Chris countered that we couldn't really discuss that, as it was subject to a confidentiality clause. They didn't relent, and asked who paid the settlement figure. We explained that the payment came out of the show's fees, and would they mind not asking any more questions about that? They backed off.

Delve said that he would like the report to look at *Verre*, our restaurant in the Dubai Creek Hotel, my partnership with Aramark, the American contract caterers, and the Gordon Ramsay Skills Centre. This last one really had me. That was the title of our in-house training department, and raising that broke the pattern that had begun to emerge. I explained that the skills centre was not a revenue stream, and, therefore, quite irrelevant to their enquiries.

They must have accepted that because they moved on to our private dining facility, wanting confirmation that we recorded the income separately and, more to the point, what assurances could we give that the income had been recorded in full? Of course our income was recorded in full. Moreover, just to pee thoroughly over their smoking bonfire, Chris pointed out that, in all our hotel restaurants, the owners of the hotel had the right of access to all our sales records since their income from us was based on the restaurants' turnovers, so that, in a way, they were all double-audited.

It was becoming clear that these two pen-pushers had done their homework and they weren't just being nosy. They asked questions that continued to hang in the air, however they were answered. They would ask a question, get a straight answer and just scribble notes, saying nothing. This was a clever technique because you felt like telling them more about the circumstances just to get some sort of confirmation from them that they believed what you said. In the back of my mind was the advice I had once received from Chris during some litigation: 'Just answer the question as briefly as possible and say nothing more.' I was terrible at this. I wanted to paint the whole picture in 3-D and in colour. Yet, however much I rambled, no appreciation of what I was telling them became apparent. They would just scribble more.

They moved on to a comparison between our operations at The Connaught and Claridge's. They had clearly looked at our filed accounts because they were asking about turnover in relation to staffing numbers and the comparative size of the two restaurants. How, they wanted to know, could The Connaught, with 138 staff, only serve a sixty-five-seater restaurant, whereas Claridge's, with 125 staff, served 125 seats. They seemed to be thinking that The Connaught 'employed' a large number of phantom staff, and that there must be a payroll with fictitious names and salary payments going to bank accounts owned by ourselves. Good try, boys, but that is not the way we operate. The Connaught may only have a sixty-five-seater restaurant, but, within the hotel, we run the whole food and beverage operation, including room service, the bars, the staff canteen and three private dining rooms.

After what seemed like over three hours of this interrogation, my arse was so paralysed that I was past caring, until they suddenly asked the most extraordinary question, given the conversation so far. Sifter said that normally, at this stage, they would ask for a payment on account to demonstrate cooperation and to keep the ongoing interest charge to a minimum. However, he continued, he appreciated that there had been no significant amounts of actual liability established but he wanted us to know that a payment on account should be considered over the coming weeks. They were about to depart and it was agreed that the 'report' should be ready within three to four months. We agreed that they had been courteous and that the meeting had been conducted in a satisfactory way. We agreed that this was the case, since they asked. I was thinking that I had entered a whole new world, and I was going to be more than happy to leave this to Chris to deal with while I got on with my real life.

Confident that it would all go away within four months, I bid my farewells to the two intrepid travellers as they started back for Leeds. Had I known, at that stage, that the report would take a further two and a half years, I wouldn't have been quite so big in my goodbyes and good wishes for a safe return journey.

Over the coming months, Chris became my interrogator. It is he who now tried to build up a picture of my early finances. He had hired a specialist tax lawyer who knew the Code 8 scenario back to front. And surprise, surprise. What was he in a previous life? An Inland Revenue tax inspector from the Special Compliance Office. Chris got Tana searching the loft for a million early records. Luckily, Tana is a hoarder, and boxes of old bills, bank statements and cheque stubs came rolling out, all to be sent over to the office for closer inspection, put into order and deciphered for 'earnings', 'TV fees' and 'trav exps'. It all had to be taken apart with care, and backup documents had to be found. This might have been great fun, except for one thing: who has the time to be fucking about with the history books? This all happened years ago, and we had a busy life. Fucking busy. I felt sorry most of all for Chris, who was now surrounded by a daily blizzard of paper, trying to tie everything up. It was going to take for ever, and, in the meantime, it was interfering with his day job.

One thing was becoming crystal clear: make sure all your past records are in order, filed and ready for such an eventuality. Otherwise, this is what will happen to you.

We received a letter summarizing the points brought to our attention at the earlier meeting. There were forty separate points, and while that looked containable, there were other requests for all bank statements for all accounts and all documents relating to the purchase and sale of all houses, flats and cars. What was more harrowing was that the enquiry was now extended to all the companies within the Gordon Ramsay group.

Then there was an interesting development. Our accountants received a letter from none other than Mr Delve, announcing that he was leaving the Revenue and starting a 'proper job'. He was joining one of the larger accounting firms that specializes in tax work. It occurred to Chris that if he was joining this firm, they must be good. Clearly, Mr

Delve, before taking up his proper job, would have worked with this firm when they were representing clients with Revenue problems, and, for sure, they must have been good to attract him. Within a few days, we had appointed this firm to handle the enquiry, and, in a relatively short period, we were paying out fees all over the place. Mr Delve could play no further part in this, and I hoped that Mr Sifter wouldn't get lonely.

Slowly, innocent discrepancies started to appear. Nothing too serious, but unexplained items showed up in my bank accounts, and when I looked to see what was on the counterfoil of the paying-in book, it was blank. It was just an indication that, at the time, I didn't take all this too seriously, which, in retrospect, was a fucking big mistake. The enquiry went up a notch, and it was now called Code 9. This was supposed to frighten me because words like 'fraud' were mentioned. It did frighten me. As these blank pages appeared and I could not explain where the money came from, I would have to pay 40 per cent tax plus interest and penalties. Not only that, but I had to start paying money over straight away, on account. How long, I wondered, would this all go on?

The new firm handling the enquiry, in effect, became the Revenue. They were not going to let the slightest thing escape, as it would reflect on them, and they were having a whale of a time. The deeper they went into my affairs, and now into my company affairs, the bigger their fees. They had every expert to hand – a VAT expert, a PAYE expert, a share-valuation expert and an expert in sending me bills. As I once said to Edwina Currie at a rather more frivolous time, 'You shagged our prime minister, and now you are trying to shag me from behind.' This is exactly what it felt like, with perfect strangers asking me if my kids had bank accounts and how much I gave Tana for housekeeping. Are you sure that there are no hidden bank accounts that you need to tell me about, and what's your inside leg measurement? At the moment, pretty big, as there is no more effective passion-killer than a jolly good frolic in the hay with the Inland Revenue.

If this was going to give the companies a good health check, then that would be fine. With the exception, perhaps, of a few airline tickets that should have been paid for privately, rather than by the company, there was little to get excited about. That's the difference between my private finance and that of the companies.

So, two and a half years later, a report was put together, pages and pages of it, and off it went to Mr Sifter and his new companion. In time they read it, assessed it, checked it, and started to suggest figures that were not unlike the country's defence budget. We argued. They counter-argued, and, one day, a figure was agreed. Most of the amount due was already sitting in the Revenue's bank account. All I felt was relief that they had gone away, and a burning conviction that never will anything be more important than complete, explainable accounts. Just in case they come back.

I was with a colourful billionaire one night during the enquiry, and I can't remember how it came up, but we started talking about tax enquiries. He told me how he had been 'done by a similar raiding party' some years back, and after six years of enquiry, he wrote them a cheque for £6 million. That made my experience seem small beer at the time, but I can see that these Revenue boys keep their ears to the ground. Once they are in, they will find something, believe me.

The lesson from all this? Whatever size your enterprise, get the accounting done properly. It will cost you hundreds of pounds that way, and will just be part of the everyday discipline. Do it the other way, and it will not only cost you thousands, but it will bring disruption and heartache, and it will take your eye completely off the ball. I remember when Chris started to give me two cheques for my intellectual property earnings. One would be for 60 per cent and the other would be for 40 per cent. Attached to the 60 per cent would always be a Post-It note, saying, 'This is yours. Do what you want with it.' The other also had a note, which simply read, 'Not yours, but look after it in a high-interest deposit account until it's called for. You get the interest, they get the money.'

And just in case you think that this was all one big joke, let me tell you how seriously we have taken this. Mr Delve now works for me. He is our full-time compliance director. Against all the odds, he turned out to be an OK guy who has supported Chelsea all his life, but has never had the chance to see them play. He will now.

CHAPTER THIRTEEN

THERE ARE GIRLS IN MY SOUP

*Ignore women in your team at
your peril. And at your loss.*

THERE WAS ALWAYS banter about the part women have
played in the kitchen. Like vegetarians, they were always
fair game for a cheap quip that brings mailbags of letters
from outraged Penelope of Cheltenham or newspaper art-
icles about my thoughts on women who can only work three
weeks in every month. All silly stuff, and I have learned the
hard way that you ignore women in business at your peril.
I have met some who can knock their male equivalents into
a cocked hat, and they have sometimes played a key role
in my business life, as well as in the family home.

Angela Hartnett was the first example I came across of
someone who, in her view of life and making a success of
herself, was tenacious, capable and determined to put aside
the war of the sexes unless she could turn it to her advantage. She joined me in the early *Aubergine* days in Park
Walk, and somehow she withstood all the pressures that
were exerted on her during a seventeen-hour day. It was she

who demanded equal terms, not to make her life easier, but to stop me from sending her home early before the end of service. She was fucking desperate to learn, and always seemed able to absorb lessons that went well beyond the kitchen. She laughed at money and yet wanted to make it. It never ruled her life, but became an intrinsic part of it. I include her here briefly because she is such a great example of a businesswoman, but the detail is best provided in the story of her involvement in *The Connaught*.

You will recall the story about the City bankers who blew £44,000 on wine at *Pétrus*. It hit the southern hemisphere newspapers and then spread around the world in minutes. This was all very well, but it could have looked as though we had sold our guests down the river, which would have fucked our reputation as well as theirs, and although everyone in the company was sworn to secrecy, the identity of the bankers soon got out. The person who had to bear the brunt of getting the story right was Jo Barnes, a tall, elegant woman who has, as they say, been brought up well. She is that rare female who should have been born a man so that she wouldn't have to waste so much time fighting her corner in a man's world, where she so rarely lost.

I first came across Jo in 2000 when she was running the PR department of Quadrille Publishing – a department of one, that is. Alison Cathie, the managing director of Quadrille and another example of a driven woman in a money world, had brought Jo to *Royal Hospital Road* for lunch and to introduce her to the early world of Gordon

Ramsay. I had had a rather desperate time with Conran Octopus, who had given up on me after only two books, and now I had moved to Quadrille, who were about to publish *A Chef for All Seasons*. The two of them ate and said hello, and, to be honest, I don't remember much else, looking back, but for Jo, apparently, it was a defining moment. In later years, she said that, there and then, she ceased working on any other authors and just concentrated on my stuff. Obviously, the dish of the day had appealed to her.

Jo's commercial upbringing had been through the ranks of Big Publishing, where she had helped launch books on everything from interiors and gardening to self-help and white witches. But her real passion was for publicizing cookery books and the chefs who produced them. During her time at Headline, and then Quadrille, she had worked with such 'luminaries' as Worrall Thompson, Torode, Novelli and Carluccio.

She worked tirelessly on my titles, and sales soared, as in from 5,000 to 50,000. Alison, at our rare chance meetings, looked like the cat who got the cream. Jo, in the meantime, began to establish herself as part of the Gordon Ramsay brand. She organized the book tour for *A Chef for All Seasons*, and, in those days, we had the extravagance of being able to devote two weeks to book signings, with visits to every major city. She crammed in these book signings from early morning to late in the evening, and the books just flew off the shelves. I remember the first occasion when Jo called round to see my PA in the Fulham shoebox to talk through some details. Chris wasn't so involved in the publishing side in those early days, and, being tucked around the corner of the office, was only able to hear the demanding tones of Jo, as she commandeered the poor, wilting PA. Chris could stand it no longer and he went round to see what Boadicea, Queen of the Iceni, really looked like. 'Who the fuck are you?' was probably the introductory greeting, but, from that moment on, he knew that in front of him was someone special. In the years to come, there were occasional screaming matches, usually on a Friday afternoon, but they were always followed by make-up lunches. As Jo would say, 'If he doesn't kill me, he will make me stronger.'

And then Jo did something really dumb. She left Quadrille and joined a PR firm specializing in restaurants. She desperately wanted to work in restaurant PR, rather than book marketing, and she saw this as an opportunity to make the break. What she hoped for was that she could take on the Gordon Ramsay account, and I am sure her new employer was very happy for her to do that. I had already engaged a PR agency for the opening of *Royal Hospital Road* and *Pétrus*, and, of course, it was their opinion that the success of the two restaurant openings was mainly down to them. I used to get totally pissed off at the end of each month, when their retainer bills arrived with 1,000 taxi receipts, photocopying charges and 'extras' attached. These PR ghosts never really seemed to do much that was tangible. I think that Jo had spotted this, and was clever enough to see that if people like Chris and myself were to be convinced about the need for a PR agency, then a very different approach was needed.

Jo turned up at the office one day with her new boss, who seemed to consider that pitching up in jeans was the order of the day. As their presentation with its promises and strategies unwound, I could see a degree of unease gradually spreading across Jo's face. They said their piece, waved goodbye and went off, while I considered if they were for us. They needn't have bothered. Jo was the one I wanted, and she was clearly uncomfortable with her new partners, which is why she did something much smarter than before. She started up on her own.

She set up Sauce Communications with her lifelong friend Nicky Hancock, with just £4,000 of their collective savings. They moved into an unheated office above an old print factory in Arsenal, and asked if they could represent me. The agreement to entrust her with our PR networking came into effect immediately, which must have given Jo some reassurance with a monthly cheque from the beginning. I am rather ashamed to say that we were probably hard in our negotiation over the fee, but Jo grabbed it, and since that day, that whole side of our business has been handled by the ever-growing Sauce Communications. In those early start-up days, their desks came from the damaged goods bay at IKEA and the office heating was a Puffa jacket for each of them. When they advertised for their very first employee, they put a small ad in the *Guardian* and had over 600 replies. Amy, the girl they took on then, is still there and is a formidable Number Three. It was she who met Mark Sargeant, my chef de cuisine at *Gordon Ramsay at Claridge's*, and married him. Now Sauce has been going for six years and there are fifteen employees. It is, without doubt, the most successful name in restaurant PR, and they have recently diversified into food and drink PR, and I have no doubt that they will succeed. Such is my confidence in them that, two years ago, Gordon Ramsay Holdings bought 10 per cent of the shareholding. We would have been happy to buy a larger holding, but Jo and Nicky would not budge past 10 per cent.

Some of the stories Jo handled for us have become milestones: the day I had a red moment when A. A. Gill brought Joan Collins to *Royal Hospital Road* and I asked them to leave; the time when those bankers blew £44,000 on wine at *Pétrus*; the £100 white truffle pizzas from *maze*; and the outrage we felt when the then CEO of the AA demoted *Pétrus* from five stars to four (a decision later reversed) – these were all stories that would make any PR firm quake. Not Jo Barnes. She just ensured that the stories found the right ears, and the column inches followed.

Her media strategy for the launch of the various restaurants was to let the individual chefs retain their own identities. They each were a branch stretching from the Gordon Ramsay tree, and Sauce worked hard at generating profiles for them all. When Angela Hartnett opened at *The Connaught*, she was followed by two film crews and featured heavily in the BBC's *Trouble at the Top*. She, along with Stuart Gillies, Jason Atherton and Marcus Wareing, have all enjoyed high media profiles, with television appearances and book deals to match. This has been a clever strategy, as it has meant that the Gordon Ramsay brand has been built without dilution of the name, and no one has ever had to pretend that I am cooking in 100 kitchens at once.

What is it that has made Jo so outstanding and successful? I think it is a great deal more than tenacity, grit and determination. These are everyday requirements. What Jo has been so successful in doing is understanding what the client's brand demands, even if the client himself hasn't realized it. She has a blend of humour, seriousness and passion for the company and for us. I have seen her in tears of frustration and I have seen her jump through hoops to make things work.

Jo reminds me of another one of these amazingly determined women, Lyndy Redding. Lyndy became known to me through her company, Absolute Taste, which is an event-organizing firm that literally started in the pit lane of Formula One. Ron Dennis had seen her supplying catering for a key sponsor, and when that came to an end, he persuaded her to take over hospitality for McLaren and went into partnership with her in her own catering company. And so she made that heady transition from chef to businesswoman. She is dynamic and enthusiastic, to a huge degree, and I love to hear that our two companies are gradually doing more events together. Like Jo, Lyndy is self-effacing and anxious only to get on with the job, whether it's organizing my fortieth birthday bash or supplying luxury dining for private airline companies. She's the sort of woman who just tears down the barriers that supposedly prevent a woman from achieving whatever it is that she has set out to do.

Back in 2002, we were staging the final of the college section of our annual scholar award in the kitchens of *Pétrus*. This is open to all young chefs already working in the UK, and involves various stages that lead to regional cook-offs and, eventually, a grand finale at which the Gordon Ramsay Scholar Award is handed to the outstanding talent of the year. Alongside all the young working chefs are students still at college, who are allowed to enter a special category, and the winner gets a wild card to compete with the other regional winners. It's a great jamboree, but fucking hard work, and on this occasion, we had drafted in a young woman to act as invigilator. Her name was Gillian Thomson.

Towards the end of the evening, everyone went upstairs for the presentation. Chris, in his normal obtuse way, did the reverse of everyone else and went downstairs, only to find Gillian washing up and clearing the kitchen. He asked her what the fuck she was doing. There were kitchen porters to do that, and, anyway, why didn't she go upstairs and enjoy the party? Again, it was that defining moment. We were being presented with a 23-year-old future star who was not interested in the glitz of the occasion, just the opportunity to do something properly. Within a couple of days, she was offered a job, and although I have no recollection of the job specification, it didn't really matter. We just wanted her on board.

Gillian's great talent was to take an overview of what was needed and then deal with it. We had just opened *Gordon Ramsay at Claridge's*, and after months of planning, staffing, purchasing and arse-kicking, we had not only put together a formidable restaurant, but had established a format for the future. This was the format that Gillian was to embrace in opening *The Connaught, The Savoy Grill, Boxwood, Pétrus*, when it moved to The Berkeley, *maze* and then our global offerings, starting with New York. Each time she would fine-tune it and recognize that each location was a little different, with a particular profile to be considered.

The various openings were just that. Once the honeymoon of a launch was over, it was down to the serious business of operating the restaurants, and in the fullness of time, Gillian built an operations team that was second to none. She was everywhere in an amazingly non-invasive way, and could pick things up quickly and add them to her territory. I remember hearing from Chris how he had taken her into his annual insurance renewals meeting with our broker. This is review time for all the insurance policies for each of the companies. The profile of our business changes throughout the year, and it is these changes that have to be reassessed. Chris and the broker were in earnest discussion for over two hours and were just drawing the meeting to a close when Gillian asked why there was no insurance provision for the old *Pétrus* restaurant, which was now operating as *Fleur*. There must have been an arse of a silence before the two of them had no option but to admit that they had forgotten all about it. The following year, the business of insurance renewal was taken over and handled by Gillian.

Gillian is now 29 and runs the whole operational centre. She has developed a team of Gillians, each responsible for a separate area of activity. I think of her as someone who looks after your interests. In turn, she will expect you to do the same, and by that I don't mean that she is ever-looking for more money, BUPA, longer holidays, a big title and that whole fucking nine yards. Chris tells me that if you meet three people in your working life like her, you are just plain lucky, so don't ever lose her. She's not entrepreneurial. She just knows about routine, discipline and keeping the pressure up on hapless fuckers who don't perform. When new people join us, I sometimes explain that they will start off loathing Gillian. She will watch you – not as a mother hen, but as a hawk. Once you begin to win her respect, this will change and there will be a reluctant softening. No one who's been with her for any length of time will hold any resentment, and everyone has come round to her way of working. Become one of her lieutenants and the mother-hen syndrome ensures a protection that will repel the hardest bastards, who are then introduced to the word 'meek'. I have, on a couple of occasions, seen how she can deal with wobbly general managers in the hotels, and I don't exaggerate when I say she can frighten the living shit out of you.

Early on, when Chris and I had realized that we had someone special, we took her out to dinner. I have no idea why, but we went all the way over to *Riva*, in Barnes. I just remember seeing Gillian looking at the menu, working out what she wanted to eat, working out what to make of us. We had taken her out to tell her that she was doing well and that we had great hopes for her, but that we needed to smooth off some of her rough. Fuck me. Were we swimming in a dangerous current. She just sat back, took it on the chin, and carried on eating the fricassee of chicken and nodding her agreement to any character rearrangement that we required. Except, of course, Gillian would never change. She didn't need to. Scottish, brash, don't fuck with me, I've been there before – but at the mention of her grandpa or her disabled uncle, she suddenly develops a need to adjust her contact lenses, and it was three years before I realized that she didn't wear any. Men are so stupid sometimes. I should know.

It's an odd thing how women are always popping up in our workforce. We have some real talent in our kitchens, and in the offices, I think 80 per cent of the staff are female. It makes absolutely no difference to me, in spite of the daft reports that end up in the newspapers, and even maternity leave has become part of everyday commercial life. As for paternity and parental leave, well, that's going to take some getting used to.

CHAPTER FOURTEEN

I BUY A HOUSE

Dealing with home affairs can require the
same discipline as the workplace.
But remember, builders are
on a different planet.

WHAT IS THE FIRST thing people think about buying when
they suddenly begin to make money? A pound to a penny,
they look to buy a car. The only requisite for this purchase
is that it's different from any car that they have previously
owned, in that it has to be new, fast, big and whatever else
is needed for this very public announcement that things are
on the up. That is exactly what it is: an announcement on
wheels. It means that you have arrived, and there is nothing better in the world than a fucking wonderful jam jar to
broadcast to everyone about your success. But it's not just
an announcement to the public. Even better than being a
total arsehole and showing it off to anyone who will look
is the big, thrusting turn-on you get when you drive it. The
car dealer carried out the introduction, and the marriage
was arranged, witnessed by half a dozen signatures on the
HP form, but now the true seduction begins. The smell of
leather gives me as big a hard-on as the sound of the V12

under the bonnet. The willingness of this sex-on-wheels to do exactly as you command within a nanosecond of your foot pushing pedal to the metal, and the added purr of pleasure from your new partner, confirm your passion, as the fuel explodes somewhere deep in the white-hot power-house.

Fidelity in these metallic marriages was, however, not my strong point. The physical pleasure was such that I always imagined that around the corner would be something faster and more fulfilling. Daft, I know, but totally compulsive – and expensive. Cars were bought, tried and replaced. Every time this happened, I would lose money, as the value suddenly plunged and I had to pay off the HP man, with his quaint phrase, 'agreement redemption'.

There was, however, something really nagging me. All this work, this gathering fame, and what had I really got? As money came in, it went straight out, not even on all the inconsequential things that get bought (well, there were the cars), but on the business. The restaurants had a voracious appetite for new capital as we expanded, and here we were, living in rented houses again, no longer on the property ladder. We had bought our first flat and sold it. We had moved out of bricks and mortar, admittedly turning a profit, but that had gone straight into the company's coffers.

I was beginning to resent this. I was beginning to resent Chris. It seemed to me that he was responsible for this state of affairs. He had already had his Mayfair flat and whatever else for years, and here I was, working my bollocks off and going home to someone else's house. We had our moments. and give Chris his due, he knew what was gnawing at me. I also knew he was right. The business had to come first, and it was still early-growth days. We were self-financing and hardly owed the bank anything. Nevertheless, I wasn't happy about this state of affairs, and I was looking around to change things. What I never imagined, but was about to learn, was that house-hunting, house-purchasing and house renovation need every bit as much sweat, imagination and attention to detail as running a restaurant.

Once you set your mind on something like buying a house, it takes you over, and, as happens in life, what seemed like the right opportunity suddenly presented itself. We needed a big house. We needed a big garden for the kids, and we needed a big garage for my cars. We also needed a big statement of what we were doing and where we were in life. There, in the middle of Wandsworth, right on the common, was this big house that had spent the last thirty years of its 100-year life as four flats. Each floor was self-contained, and it was clear to anyone that nothing had been spent on this building for a very long time.

Tana rang the agent and arranged to meet outside the house. A Sloane pitched up in a Mini, with the syrupy voice of someone who was convinced that her 'pedigree' would add thousands to the price of the house. Together they spent an hour going through the building, flat by flat, observing four households and the way the occupants lived. There were cats, overflowing bins, unmade beds and a stale smell of diluted pee throughout. There was paper peeling from the walls, skirtings painted in puce and unshaded lights hanging from the ceilings. The communal garden was wide and long, and hadn't seen a lawnmower since they started to put engines in them. Worse, the garden had become a dumping ground for an unwanted fridge, two prams and an assortment of filthy, rotting settees. By then, the afternoon was getting dark, it had been raining most of the day, and the leaves had long since fallen off the branches. In a moment, on that dank, depressing November afternoon, Tana knew that this would become the family home, and summoned me to see it.

I have to say that we are very good at looking beyond the peeling paper and cat shit. We knew at once that it had everything we needed – space, potential – and no one else would want it. So we thought.

Sloane had laid out the hurdles that we faced if we wanted it. We assured her that we wanted it and would immediately start the process. The one thing that I had learned in the kitchens was that when things need doing, you need to ensure that there are people around who can make them happen. If you can't do something, then find someone who can. So Tana got on the phone to Chris. Persuade him that this house is the one for us, and we are home and dry, so to speak. Tana calls her father and asks if he could spare an hour to see something. He thinks it's another car, but because it's his daughter calling, he agrees to meet at Wandsworth.

'Where the fuck is Wandsworth?' he asks.

He can be so annoyingly small-minded sometimes.

'Dad, just get in your car and head south from Fulham. The office will still be there when you get back.'

He arrives looking perplexed, and Tana launches into her spiel.

They pick their way through the flats, cats and detritus, as Tana explains our embryonic plans. She can see that he is intrigued, but she keeps an ace up her sleeve until they start to walk through the urban wasteland of the garden. At the end is a long wall with a door in it, and Tana has a key. She unlocks the door and opens it to reveal the most amazing secret garden. All eighteen acres of it. This is the communal garden shared by ten neighbouring properties and walled all the way around. There is a running track, a tennis court and beautiful woodlands, shady nooks and 100-foot trees. This cannot still be London. But it is. Chris has been passed the ball, and, as he looks around, he can see that there are high expectations among the crowd. All he has to do is run for the line.

'How much?' he asks.

There is one of those pauses. Not exactly pregnant – more like waiting for the result of a hastily bought Boots dipstick. Tana explains that there appears to be more interest than she had thought. So much interest, in fact, that the agent, who is acting for all four flat-owners, has put the sale out to tender. This means that all you get is a guide price and you have to bid. The highest bid secures the house, and no one, apart from the agent, will ever know what the other bids contained. The guide price is £2,750,000, and I am looking at a debt that I can hardly imagine. Put 2,750,000 £1 coins in a line and they will stretch for nearly 40 miles. The other fact that Chris will need to know is that the bids have to be in by the following Tuesday, and it's Thursday today. No pressure, then.

The good thing about Chris is that, once he's got the bit between his very white teeth, he really moves. He asks how much we want the house. We nod our heads like plastic dogs on the parcel shelf of a car. In that case, he tells us, bid £2,850,010. That's £100,000 higher than the guide price and an extra £10 in case someone else does the same. The next stage is to call the bank. Ever since that fiery little Scot Iain Stewart had paved the way to *Royal Hospital Road*, we had followed him as he jumped ship from Bank of Scotland to the head of private banking at the little-known bank Singer & Friedlander. Chris tells him that we need to know that £2,750,000 will be available in the event that we are successful with our bid. Iain asks how much we are going to spend on the property and where the money is coming from. Chris tells him £100,000 and that it is already in the bank. Is it fuck. Iain goes away and holds an emergency credit committee meeting. For him, it could be good business, and he is the one person who knows that it will be good for the bank.

The following day we get the nod, and the tender price goes in as Chris had suggested. We now have two days to wait and see if we have been successful. It's not an easy feeling. If we are successful, we have a house that we can't live in and doesn't generate any money, and a debt that stretches 40 miles down the road. If we are unsuccessful, at least we know that the bank is ready to lend us, what seems to me, massive sums of money. Tana calls Sloane on Tuesday at 10 a.m., only to find that she has a day off. So much for her enthusiasm. Sloane's boss calls immediately afterwards to say that they should know by 4 p.m. We wait.

Eventually we get the call to say that we have been successful and that it's all ours, once the contracts have been exchanged. I am ecstatic and scared shitless. There is also the feeling that any player in this tender game must have. Did we overpay, or did we, as we would like to think, just squeeze in with exactly the price that was needed? Maybe the £10 was enough. This is something that we shall never know, and all that matters now is whether or not this will be the right house for us.

Within the next few days, papers fly around for signature, and the first shock hits me. The house has sold for £2,850,010, and the government holds its hand out for an additional 4 per cent. What a fucking cheek. £114,000 for nothing. £114,000 for the government to waste. To pay for this house, I have already had to pay 40 per cent tax. Clearly, that wasn't enough. Now I have this stamp duty and God knows how much VAT on the restoration of this pile. No wonder people with real money disappear to Monaco.

By the time completion takes place, we are ready to send in the wrecking crew. A self-employed Polish army, with each soldier earning £120 a day, plus an overseer, starts work on removing years of other people's lives. The skips just continue filling up, one after the other, until the building is stripped of every recognizable trapping and each room is as bare as a cave. The floorboards then come up, and suddenly there is this four-storey skeleton awaiting its new body. Before the transplant starts, I become involved with a set of professional people who will plan, draw, prepare building applications, control costs and manage the project. I say I want a window somewhere, and off they go to arrange it. An architect, a quantity surveyor and a structural engineer all come together, and I feel that control over this project is slipping away from me. The £100,000 that Chris told the bank would be spent on the house has attracted another nought. That's what happens in life when something that you do is outside your area of knowledge. I hate it because already I can see that there are varying levels of skill within the workforce. Worse, the project manager has only little balls, and when a line of tiles is not straight, he says nothing. When the rendering on an outside wall has been done by a first-timer, I have to threaten to bring down my pastry chef, who could do a better job, before anything is done about it.

The restoration of this house is a lesson for life. Even when something is way off your screen, don't just leave everything to the 'professionals'. They may have the whole fucking alphabet after their names, but do they also have the words 'common sense' inscribed somewhere? Nine times out of ten, probably not – they just imagine that their training and advanced knowledge are sufficient to blow their boats through any storm. This is not good enough in my book, and the sooner you realize who you're dealing with and find a clear-thinking replacement, the better. If they have some lateral thinking capacity, even better. That's why my favourite space-race story will always be NASA's quest for the pen that propels ink in zero gravity. After a billion dollars of taxpayers' money and the commitment of huge resources, they managed to come up with a workable answer, whereas the Russians thought the problem through and used pencils.

There is nothing wrong with the 'professionals'. Don't get me wrong on this. They are a vital part of most projects. But make sure you have the right ones. If they are ahead of their game, then keep them for life.

Bit by bit, brick by brick, things start to come together, and although I see these fucking irritating problems, the house gradually takes shape. The process takes over a year, and I visit it each week to chart the slow, steady progress. I'm amazed to find that, whenever the project is mentioned in one of the tabloids, I receive a load of mail offering every service you can imagine, from aluminium guttering to personalized drip-mats for the bar.

By August 2003, the house is ready for us to move into. It is now a house, but it will take another three years to become a home. All I have to do now is pay for it.

At the back of the house was a bizarre concrete bunker, and although it was top of the list for demolition, its presence did give me the idea of building a commercial kitchen at the back, where I could carry out much of the photographic and filming work involved in my books and television programmes. A planning application was submitted, and I guess it was difficult for anyone to complain when I was proposing a beautiful addition to replace what Prince Charles would have referred to as 'a monstrous carbuncle on the face of an old friend'. I don't know which old friend he was thinking of, but permission came through without any problems.

The design was to be modern and similar to a large conservatory, as I would need plenty of light. It was hooked up to the house for easy access, and was built in three months. I equipped it as though it were one of my restaurant kitchens, with a beautiful, chrome-plated Rorgue, the Rolls-Royce of stoves from France, which sat in the middle of the kitchen like an island so that it was accessible from every angle. A local kitchen firm designed the units, and suddenly the space was filled with hanging copper pans and every conceivable piece of equipment, from knife blocks to mandolins. It looked the very essence of a dream kitchen. I gazed at the finished state and wondered if I would ever use it.

It became a complete lifesaver. It was exactly what was needed to propel me in the world of publishing and television. With cookery books, the attraction is the photography, and suddenly I had a kitchen with all the space needed to allow a professional photographer to do the job properly. The television-programme-makers wasted not a minute, and were quick to extend this 'facility' to include the garden, where I suddenly found myself rearing turkeys and pigs for Channel 4's *F Word*.

In the end, it is impossible to separate home and work completely, however much you try. Building homes and building a restaurant business both need you to keep your wits about you. Particularly if there are builders involved.

CHAPTER FIFTEEN

PUBLIC FLOGGINGS

Keep an eye on what goes on in big finance
for the heads-up on greed, ineptitude and
the general disregard for Joe Soap. It can be
a lesson for us all.

ONE GREAT ADVANTAGE that small firms have over their larger brothers is their ability to change course quickly when necessary. Things go wrong, markets change, and the smaller the company, the more chance there is for an early alteration in course. I think of the quarter-of-a-million-ton oil tanker that takes three miles to stop, compared with the manoeuvrable tug, which has all the flexibility to deal with immediate change. But the tanker, as it puts on the brakes or starts to turn, pulls along everything in its wake, and is unable to help the flotilla in its way. In the same way, big corporations and government bodies will push all obstacles out of the way, resulting in some fucking great injustice. Invariably, they are driven by one of three motives: money, political need or stupidity. Sometimes all three combine for a star turn.

As I have grown up a bit, I stop getting furious and try to put together in my mind the backdrop that can make these travesties happen. It is by doing this that you can work out an alternative route, and therein lies the craziest situation. There is always another route, another way to solve the problem, an alternative to the tanker knocking the shit out of everyone. But big corporations rarely do alternatives.

I am one of a party of seventy-five on a flight returning from the Continent. We have just had a family do, a wonderful weekend with all the people I want in my life. We are all in a queue, looking slightly worse for wear, as the previous night had been a party that had strayed way past the midnight hour, and Krug '90 had been as plentiful as water flowing from a fountain. Gradually we all get scanned, checked, tagged and seated in the holding area, waiting for the plane to be turned around, ready for the return flight. That is, all of us except five of our group, who hold perfectly valid tickets, have arrived on time, but no longer have seats. Their prepaid, valid tickets have been resold on the chance that they might not have turned up. And the plane takes off without them. Three of the party are a husband, a wife and a small daughter. I say 'small', but probably aged three or four, and there are no further flights until the following day.

I don't hear the full story until the following evening, when I get the shakedown on what took place at the hands of the carrier's ground crew. My friends felt that they were treated badly and that the airline couldn't have given a damn. This overbooking is a scenario that happens every day, and the only way to handle its victims is to ignore them and treat them as irritating, annoying airport vagrants. I thought about the rare times when we have fucked up with a reservation for one of our restaurants and a party turns up for a table that somehow doesn't exist. It has happened, believe me, and what do we do about it? Well, what we do is try to save the day. Our name is already spoiled with an uncomfortable whiff of incompetence and disappointment, and what we know is that you can make friends with a fire truck. The house is ablaze, and what it needs is extinguishing. Put on a fireman's uniform and walk past the fire because it's your lunch break, and you are dead. Grab a bucket and start throwing water over the blaze, and you are seen to be God's little helper. So we don't stand in front of our guests and say, 'Tough luck, arseholes,' we solve the problem, even if it costs us ten taxis, an escort to an alternative restaurant and a bill that never gets presented.

So I wrote to the then head of this airline. I explained that I had recently been rather embarrassed, having spent £20,000 on a return trip for seventy-five friends and family, that some of the party had had to give up their seats because the flight was overbooked. This was a personal letter to the Big Dick of the airline, and I never received a reply. Now I don't expect a big shot who is busy playing aeroplanes to pick up the phone and say sorry but I did think that maybe some PA was squirrelled away with the sole job of writing apologies to what must be growing unrest from unsatisfied customers. Nope. That same culture of ignoring the poor

fucker stretches right across the board. You can only imagine that the board is where it originated, because the
response I got was so minimal that it completely passed me
by. I thought back to the husband, wife and small daughter who had asked for help to be put up in a hotel overnight
and had been told that the only hotel was on the other side
of the city. No doubt that was the only cheap hotel that this
airline could extend to. Otherwise you are on your own,
and that is exactly what they were told. There was no offer
of compensation, although there were provisions for this
eventuality laid down in the foggy annals of air travel.

Eventually, I understand, some recompense was made, a
cheque for a few hundred pounds to the family, and nothing to the other victims because they were too embarrassed
to make a claim. No apology ever arrived. It accordingly
became our company policy to avoid flying with that airline
at every possible opportunity. This is the big fucking problem with public companies, and I look to the CEOs and
supportive chairmen to change this anal disregard for their
passengers. What it needs is a government to step in and say
that if a seat is booked and paid for, then it's yours, irrespective of whether you turn up or not. After all, if theatres or
restaurants started 'overselling', they wouldn't last two
minutes. In the airline industry it has just become accepted,
and every time anyone raises their voice, an airline repre-
sentative trots out the usual line about how that would
force up the price of tickets. So the practice is allowed to
continue.

The real problem is that this practice is everywhere, just in case you think I'm homing in on one particular airline. A very similar 'bumping' happened to Tana and myself, coming back from the USA on a different carrier. We were picked up from our hotel by the airline's limousine, which arrived at check-in two minutes late. In that two minutes, our seats had been sold and the plane was suddenly full. I had to be back in London that afternoon, and ended up buying first-class tickets from a rival and presenting the bill on my return. It was paid, but I wonder if that would have been the case if I was Mr Nobody from Planet Unknown. What a fucking nightmare when you start playing these games of greed.

It's so long ago that I can hardly recall the exact circumstances, but shortly after Tony Blair became Prime Minister, there was a sotto-voce row about a million-pound cheque for party funding from Bernie Ecclestone, which sort of crossed over at the same time as Mr Blair suggested that Formula One should get its house in order with regard to cigarette advertising. No big deal, really, except that His Nibs suggested a period of seven years to wipe away the tears and find new sponsors. Seven fucking years. There was a bit of shit flying around and the cheque was returned, but nothing much was made of it during the new PM's honeymoon, and the seven years remained.

Now, for me, politics is as exciting as electric cars, but here was a total cop-out. Why was there an impending smoking ban? Because smoking kills people. Yet Mr Blair took all those years to ban smoking in enclosed spaces. How many people died during that delay? This was the single most useless waste of time and human life. Why it happened is probably easier to answer. Money, as ever, was the key. Why it was allowed to happen is the big question. Why did we allow this prat of a PM to manipulate this delay at a time when Ireland, South Africa, Scotland, France, Italy and even his American mates across the pond legislated against the evil weed? Three years earlier we had gone no-smoking in my own restaurants, and while I fretted like a toad under a hairdryer, Chris had said that it would do us no harm. I knew he was right, and I had this confirmed when a member of staff said to me that that was the first week he went home not stinking of someone else's smoke. As the big-nosed, long-suffering Matt cartoon character from the *Daily Telegraph* arrives home after the smoking ban has finally become part of our lives, he hears his wife saying, 'I know you've been to the pub. I can't smell the smoke.'

In the early days, when we had just two restaurants, I remember receiving a call from a special tax compliance unit in London's Euston Tower. They wanted to come and examine our tronc records. The 'tronc' is the universal name that restaurants and hotels use to describe the tips received from guests, and, as such, this money belongs to the staff. In time, along came someone I took an immediate dislike to – he made my skin crawl. Once in the door, he began to call for all the tronc records, and then started quizzing our staff about how the tronc was distributed, what influence the company had in this allocation, and who handled the cash. A right little interrogation from the head of 'Operation Gourmet'. So subtle and poignant, these Revenue boys.

According to our tax policeman, we were doing nearly everything wrong. Our companies had no right to announce to a new employee what amount of tronc he or she might expect to receive. This was left to the 'troncmaster', who could be anyone on the staff and who had total control over who got what. Now *that* is a system open to abuse if ever there was one. In addition to this, tronc could never be used for breakages or credit card commissions. This meant that if the tip was included in the bill and was paid by credit card, the restaurant would have to pay the credit card commission on money that it never received. The penalty for this breach of the rules was that all tronc distribution was now subject to National Insurance Contribution, which meant an additional 12.8 per cent to be diverted from this staff money to HM Inspector of Taxes. In addition, there was a penalty of £25,000 and back interest, so, all in all, it was a nice little number for the fucking taxman.

For years we suffered under this unclear system, and Robin Hood was allowed to come and go through the employment files of each one of our restaurants, and, gradually, some pretty big cases came to light. I remember one prominent restaurant chain being subjected to a huge fine, and, inevitably, some restaurants went out of business, thanks to this inquisition. Three years later, we invited Robin back to check our records, such was our neurosis that we might still be doing something wrong. He appeared and spent three days going through 650 personnel files, looking for the one letter from the company that might indicate that it had been involved in tronc allocation. He even went up to Scotland to examine the employment files of *Amaryllis*. He drew a complete blank, and that was the last I ever saw of him. But not the last I heard of him. Within weeks it was announced that he had left the Revenue and, with the status of being the world's leading expert on the tronc system, had joined a firm of accountants to dispense knowledge at £50,000 per hour.

He had left the Revenue, and behind him remained a completely baffling system. There were never clear rules, and even hardened accountants were often bamboozled by the seriously flawed system. Gradually, the waves of protest from senior accounting bodies pushed the Revenue to take stock, and one day they cracked and admitted that there was room for change. 'Room for change' actually meant that they were wrong but wouldn't admit it, as that, of course, could lead to shedloads of claims. What about all the restaurants that, faced with a couple of hundred thousand pounds of penalties and interest charges, had to shut their doors – just because no one that drafts these rules could think in a straight line? The biggest irony of all came a few weeks later with an announcement from Robin, formerly of 'Operation Gourmet', in which he said that, as a spokesman of the accountancy practice he now worked for, he was delighted to hear that the Revenue had finally got their act together. Fuck me. How bizarre is that?

A couple of years ago, one of Chris's friends and professional advisors was killed by a car in the long-term facility at a London airport. As our accountant, Martin was one energetic, interesting, sane type of man who got a kick out of working with us and somehow dealt with numbers while still remaining human. It was a very sad occasion, and I remember how much Chris was affected by this totally pointless loss of life. Martin left a widow and four children all under the age of ten, which made the whole story increasingly poignant.

Martin was a careful man, and had headed towards the bus stop and was halfway across a marked crossing when he was hit by a car travelling at around 24 m.p.h. The advised speed limit in the area was 5 m.p.h., and there was a 60-metre strip of road leading up the crossing. Somehow, the driver didn't see Martin, hit him, and that was that. Accidents happen, and however dire the consequences, nothing is ever going to prevent their continuance. But what happened over the following years beggars belief.

Martin's widow, Sara, was approached by a legal firm, and agreed they should take on the case. They were professional operators and drew in all the right people to represent Sara. There were accident investigators, forensic accountants and a well-practised QC, together with the solicitor herself, who had the difficult job of dealing with a grieving widow and yet had to move the case forward in the interests of her client. The car driver was insured comprehensively, and it was the behaviour of the insurer that led me to wonder how on earth commercial considerations are allowed to take control to such an extent. Fortunately, Sara had the resources to keep her children at school while she battled to keep Martin's firm running. Nevertheless, her representatives sought an on-account payment from the defendant's insurers.

The moment this request was put to the insurers, they responded with a full and final offer to settle – a meagre £50,000. It wasn't a case about which they didn't know all the facts because they already had a file 10 feet high. A few months after this derisory offer, they increased it to £350,000. Today it is still not settled, but the claim has been quantified at around £3 million.

There is something very wrong about this, and it cannot be blamed on the driver. He has paid his premium and the size of the award does not concern him. He, in fact, may never even know what the final outcome will be.

Almost within a year of starting our business, I was persuaded to put in hand a pension for myself. It is clearly a tax-efficient way to bring money out of the company to help secure your future, and, as the pension salesman said, you won't even think about it for twenty years. To an extent, that's probably true, but I have seen a bit of what pensions do for people and, in the main, I'm not impressed one little bit.

The first problem is that your money is controlled in a remote, impersonal way. Everything is so vague, and you have no real idea of how your savings are likely to grow. I know that there are self-administered schemes nowadays which partially help to bridge the control factor, but surely that is not the point. Most people are not experts, and they go to pension companies in the hope that their monthly contributions will grow steadily to provide something tangible for the future. What they don't want to do, and are not equipped to do, is steer their way through the money markets. There are 'experts' out there to do that, which brings us to the second problem.

The 'experts' in the main must have been living in Outer Mongolia, judging by the appalling performances some of the funds have managed. They always seemed to be tied in to equity plans, when it was obvious that the property market was romping along with annual double-digit increases in value. Nowadays, when my young chefs come along and enquire about starting a pension, I just point to an estate agent and suggest that they buy a property to live in and, when they have done that, buy another property and let it out. At least they have some control, and even if the interest rates go up, they enjoy capital growth, which shows no real sign of contracting.

What is interesting is how defensive these pension people can be. You start to ask them why the value of your policy has risen so slowly, and they will come out with all the old tosh about the difficult equity years, and then, when equities become buoyant, they say that the new money generated will need to be used to bolster up the lean years. God help you if you are about to retire and you ask for the up-to-date value of your policy, only to find that it's so much lower than you had been led to believe that you might have to carry on working for another five years. Or depend on the State handout, which, in effect, is another pension fuck-up, judging by the pittance you get after a lifetime of paying into the Treasury's coffers. And who can you complain to?

I watched Chris a couple of years ago, planning to buy some residential property with his pension under the SIPPS rules, only to find that, six months before the scheme went live, the government did a complete U-turn and removed residential property from the area for self-administered pensions. How the government had allowed hundreds of thousands of ordinary people to be led along this path and then to have the brass neck to change track is beyond me. Not only that, but they got away with it, with little more than a few column inches of anger for a couple of days.

That's the problem when you have to deal with the corporate giants, inside and outside of government. Of all the lessons I've learned in building up a business, it's they who make me sweat most at night.

CHAPTER SIXTEEN

THE FEE-EARNERS

*Professional fee-earners are unwelcome
necessities who should be given a hard
time, but never ignored.*

I DON'T KNOW how much I have spent on professional fees over the past nine years, but it must be enough to buy out the Vatican. Having said that, my view of professional fee-earners is that, for good or bad, they become an accurate barometer of your success. They each have an area of expertise that needs greater depth and specialization as a project gets bigger. The downside about fee-earners is exactly what their name suggests: they cost shedloads of money, and sometimes I wasn't quite sure how their charges came about or, indeed, if we really needed that particular piece of advice. Sometimes I thought they just sat in a dark room and thought about sex while clocking up the hours. One thing is for certain: don't ever be tempted to do this on the cheap. Choose your advisors with care and, where possible, with glowing references from someone you know and trust. Otherwise, pound to a penny, you will get fucked, screwed and dropped from a great height.

My first experience of a fee-earner was with a bank, where it was the practice to charge an administration fee when giving a loan. When you don't know better, you readily agree to this vile practice. After all, they are being kind enough to lend this money to you. Later, I used to wonder about that. If you apply for a loan and there are all kinds of documents passing to and fro, and then you decide not to take out the loan, or the deal you need the finance for falls flat, the bank gets fuck all. So, do they add up all these fuck-all situations and then charge the successful borrowers enough to cover their earlier losses and even out the score?

Buying *La Tante Claire* from Pierre Koffmann was my first commercial experience with a lawyer. I had been involved with conveyancing solicitors when I had bought my first flat and later, when Tana and I had bought Priory Grove, but those transactions had been straightforward. You think to yourself that a couple of sheets of paper laying out the deal will be all that is needed, and perhaps someone will have the audacity to charge me a few hundred pounds for this onerous task. At this point Chris introduced me to the legal world in the form of Joelson Wilson & Co., a small firm of corporate lawyers that he had dealt with for most of his earlier life. The partner I was introduced to was Sheldon Cordell, a lively individual with a brain like a train and an energy like he was connected to the national grid. He went over the deal in simple terms, as though I was a chef or something, and then disappeared to put a couple of sheets of paper together. Chris seemed to spend for ever over at their West End offices, and couriers went backwards and forwards all day long. What the fuck could they be writing about? As the days went by, I began to think the deal was going sour, and eventually I tackled Chris about all the time-wasting.

He sat me down and explained that there might be a little more to it than just a couple of sheets of paper. There was a lease for the building that wasn't going to change, but it needed to be checked over. I mean, it might only have a week to run, or we might have to paint the building in gold every year. It's at times like these that you begin to realize that the thoroughness of the professional fee-earner is there to protect him as much as anyone else. He doesn't want to hear that, in a year's time, you are trying to sue the pants off him because he missed the small print while he was in the dark room thinking of sex. So the lease doesn't change. We just get to know about its terms. What does emerge is the purchase agreement, which lists all the things we have agreed and all the things we haven't even thought about agreeing. The draft of the purchase agreement arrives, and we go through it. It lays out who the agreement is between, what the deal is about, and then goes on to define all the terms that, without definition, might entrap the unwary. Talk about jobs for the boys. Pages of obligations, limitations and get-outs make up this fine document, and by the time we have gone through it for the first time, there are more red pen deletions and exclamation marks than on Megan's first-year cave painting. And there are other documents that have to be included.

The bank then wades in, as it is going to lend me half a million pounds. Its terms for the loan take up thirty-eight pages to define and ensure that I don't disappear when the going gets rough. Up comes the phrase 'due diligence', which seems a brain-fuck because I know Pierre Koffmann isn't going to do me over. Someone from the fee-earners' industry who knows about numbers has to come in and look over everything to do with the company. Are there debts lurking within, or dodgy deals that have somehow sidelined the taxman? Does the balance sheet stack up? Is anyone ever going to read all these findings, or is it just a document that gets stuck in a drawer, like a BUPA health check? I loved the letter of disclosure. It was like a confession, and reminded me of when a little old lady is in the dock for shoplifting and, on pleading guilty, asks for 300,000 other shoplifting offences to be taken into consideration. In effect, it clears the decks and no one can come back afterwards and say that they weren't aware you hadn't paid any VAT for the past ten years.

So, eventually we are done, and Sheldon Cordell arranges the completion meeting, where all the documents are lined up for signing. By now, I know that there will be more than just a couple of sheets of paper, but, nevertheless, I am totally gobsmacked when I see the piles of paper that need signing. But not half as gobsmacked as when the fee-earners' bills come home to roost. The final tally, when you add up the debit notes from our solicitors, the bank's solicitors, the lessor's solicitors, the due diligence people and the bank, with its administration fees, is an eye-watering kick in the goolies, amounting to nearly fifty thousand quid, and this is 1998. Fuck me pink!

Within only two years, we will have gotten used to this rather unwelcome side of commercial life, and have learned to live with our friends the fee-earners. Moreover, compared with their US counterparts, whom we have yet to meet, they are gentlemen from the bargain basement of the Salvation Army store.

Now the insurance industry is different. First of all, you have to decide if you are an insurance person or not. I know there are certain policies that are compulsory, such as Employer's Liability, in case someone gets shut in the oven, but you do have the choice of covering your arse or taking the chance yourself, in most cases. I have to say that I need to sleep at night, so there has never been any question about cover. It just has to happen, and do you know the greatest thing about this? The broker, who does everything for you, from filling in your date of birth on a proposal form for your Ferrari to holding your hand when the kitchen is on fire, charges nothing. It's all paid for by way of commission from the insurer. Now isn't that fucking great? As with all our fee-earners, Paul Harrison was brought in from Chris's earlier life. Paul is a together kind of suit who spends all day either on the golf course or poring over a desk of insurance. You could call him up on a Monday and tell him that a jumbo jet landed smack in the middle of *Gordon Ramsay at Claridge's,* wiped out the CEO of Microsoft and two billionaires, ruined the carpet and probably caused the restaurant to be closed for a few years, and he would quietly arrange for a claim form to be with you the following morning. Then he would follow the whole claim process all the way through, which is what you will need more than anything in the world. This is what a good broker is all about. Not just saving you money on the premium, but ensuring that he has placed the cover with someone who understands the bigger picture and isn't going to quibble about the small print. This discipline must run in the blood because before Paul there was Arthur, his dad, whom Chris started out with in 1970. I was four at the time and not into insurance, but you can see how, when you find the right people, you need to stick with them, just like the people who work with you. Lose them and it is nothing short of bad management, unless they have decided to become beach bums in the Maldives.

Accountants come in two sizes: they are either expensive or fucking outrageous. In the early days, we needed little more than straight auditing of the company books. This meant that they checked over what we had stuck in the computer for the last twelve months, added seasoning, such as a bit of depreciation, agreed the tax computations with the local taxman, and signed off the accounts for the year. Nice and straightforward, and it probably didn't cost an arm and a leg. Martin, who was to be tragically killed just as we began to appreciate his full value as a financial advisor, not only met our needs efficiently and on time, but had come up with the brilliant idea of an FPA, a fixed price agreement. This meant that he estimated what his auditing services would cost, divided by twelve, and we set up a standing order so that the fees didn't hurt so much and Martin's practice could eat regularly. As our needs grew during the year, the cost might rise and there would be a simple adjustment at the end of the year.

But our needs did grow, and, on a couple of occasions, we required not only highly specialized advice, but advice that had to come from someone who stood tall in the event that there was a challenge from Darth Vader or the taxman. We had one day been approached by *The Sunday Times*, who had done some digging and found us to be what they termed 'fast-track profit-makers'. They were publishing *The Top 100 Companies*, and whatever their formula for qualifying was, we came in at Number Nine. This meant that we received a glitzy piece of plastic to put on the mantelpiece and got written up in the paper. What also happened was that PricewaterhouseCoopers got into our boardroom to see what help they might be able to charge us for. Now, cynical as I might sound, they did turn up at more or less the right moment, as we had a slight problem. With the redevelopment of the house, I had managed to run up a director's loan account of a couple of million, which needed to be repaid at some stage, and preferably without having to pay 40 per cent beforehand. So my new friends PwC came up with a scheme. Now that was great, and although they charged enough to put a restaurant on the moon, compared with the saving, it was a fair return. Later, we used them again to audit our intellectual property and check over our trademarks. This meant a big bill for specialist stuff, but when they got pushy and sent in an unsolicited quote for our annual audit, even though the price was good, they were not for us.

After Martin's death, his widow, Sara, carried on the business of Smith Stewart & Co. It could not have been easy for her, with four young children to bring up, and both Chris and I were very happy to leave the auditing work with the practice. The manager who looked after the account must have lived on a diet of cardboard and distilled water, so lacking in any form of humour was he – probably a thoroughly professional auditor, but as flat as a punctured soufflé, and this brought home to me the importance of good rapport with the people who work around you. To walk into an office and have your 'good morning' returned with a grunt and no eye contact is not my idea of a happy house. There is always time to acknowledge that Someone is more important than Something, even if it takes a couple of precious minutes.

I know that Chris was beginning to feel uneasy about our sole reliance on Sara's firm, particularly as scale and tax issues began to raise their heads with our rapid growth. Had Martin been around, there would have been no problem, but that wasn't the case. Fortunately, Sara had already read between the lines and started negotiations with a medium-sized City firm of accountants by the name of

Jeffreys Henry LLP, who had shown considerable interest. With the help of Sheldon Cordell, who knew the partners well, a deal was struck, and we suddenly had Sara looking after our account, but with the backing of a firm with global associates who were to become key to our expansion. The interesting point was that, apparently, the big draw for Jeffreys was us. Now that was a real surprise, as I had wondered why a City practice would consider this move. Smith Stewart was certainly making money, from what I could gather, but their clients were made up in the main of sole traders and small firms – hardly the target of a City takeover. I know that the charismatic manager whom we had laboured under for so long had gone off to do his own thing and had trawled Smith Stewart for all its little fishes. These were the very clients who had caused Sara so much anguish. At first she was devastated to lose them, and then she realized that life would be so much better if she concentrated on us and the marketing of a restaurant accounting arm for her new partners. It was exactly the way I had learned to guard our resources. Any project that came our way had to be judged by the profit it was likely to earn in relation to the resources it took from the store at Gordon Ramsay Holdings.

Our relations with contractors in the building industry were not so straightforward. Neither Chris nor I had ever been involved in this area previously, and when it came to selecting contractors, we often had to resort to the Yellow Pages or just asked around. The early projects involved my house in Wandsworth and went on to six or seven pro-jects, most of which ended massively over-budget. The fees for the design and project management were huge, but on top of that came professional fees from the likes of quantity surveyors, structural engineers, party-wall experts and so on. Quantity surveyors whom I have talked to sell them-selves on the amount of savings they can introduce to a project, but, for these services, they forward accounts that often add an extra nought to the final project cost. In fact, the one thing all building contractors seem to manage to a spectacularly high standard is getting their bills in to me on time. It would be great to say that, thereafter, I walked away from all projects that involved building, but how could I move forward if I did that? At the time of writing, I am arranging for a firm of builders to take on our project at Heathrow's Terminal 5. We had plenty of time to get it right, but – surprise, surprise – for budgetary reasons, we ended up having to look for someone else at the last minute. This means that the building programme that should have started two weeks ago is already late. Great headline: 'Gordon Ramsay Holds Up Opening of T5.'

The biggest fee-earners are, undoubtedly, our legal ad-visors. There is virtually nothing that we do nowadays with-out their checking through the fine print. Ninety per cent of our legal instructions go to Joelson Wilson & Co., because they are simply the best, in terms of expertise and personal response, and they have the charming habit of calling Chris before submitting their bills. In doing so, they explain what

time has been spent and where duplication between the partners might have inflated the price. They adjust the bill accordingly, and then ask if that is all right. I don't think that there
has ever been a situation where their fees have taken me off
guard, and, in turn, our companies never ask to see the charging sheets. It is such a waste of time, auditing through figures,
and, at the end of the day, the agreement is nothing more
than a framework for making money, whether it's the start
of a new deal with a worldwide distribution of drinks or a
lease for a new restaurant premises. Better, therefore, to
conserve your energy for the money-making activity, rather
than arguing over a few beans.

But whatever my gripes about the size of fees in this
country, there is absolutely no one over here who can hold
a candle to what comes out of the United States of America.
There, fee-earning is a total fucking art form in which bills
become three-dimensional. The fee notes received during
the New York deal with Blackstone were such that each
monthly invoice was accompanied by sixty-four pages of
breakdown. When I say 'three-dimensional', I mean that
these sixty-four pages were so accurate that I could tell
which secretary typed which document just by the pizza
that appeared on the bill. The only reason I ever read these
fucking pages was when I needed a laugh, and when I
complained to anyone from that former colony of ours,
their reply was always the same: 'Welcome to America.'

My question, then, is, why exactly do we need fee-earners?
There are, of course, many areas of expertise, and that

cannot be denied. But I've discovered that many of these experts seek help from another level of expertise. So, for instance, when you design and build a bridge, behind all the praise lavished upon your world-renowned architectural practice for its elegant, chic and simple lines, there lurks a structural engineer who goes over all the figures and 'approves' them. You would know nothing of this until something goes really wrong. From this emerges the concept of professional insurance, and that, I guess, is what we are all paying for. Once our figures are audited, when the structural weight of a load-bearing wall has been checked and legal advice has been given, if it all goes wrong, you have paid someone to carry the can.

There are exceptions to this rule. If your load-bearing calculations go wrong and London Bridge falls down, then you are going to be sued for big numbers – but you can pass on the bill to the professionals' insurers. However, if some heavy legal advice wobbled, then you might be stuffed, because, in the legal world, there is the wonderful get-out of 'giving advice'. You can pay £600 an hour to get an opinion from a QC, but you go into court at your own peril. You have only been given advice based on one person's opinion, even though they know so much about the subject they can charge you £10 a minute.

So don't imagine that you can get by without the occasional fee-earner. You can't. Just watch them carefully until you feel that you can trust them, and then make sure that you don't let them go.

CHAPTER SEVENTEEN

NEW YORK

Sometimes what you want
will take a lot out of you.
Just be sure you want
it that much.

DID I EVER think about, dream about, obsess about opening in New York? Of course I fucking did. This city has something about it that is as magnetic to the serious restaurateur as the Statue of Liberty sticking to the outside of my fridge. I wanted to do something there, as did Chris and most of my regular customers, who asked a million times not 'Will I?', but 'When will I?' Blackstone also wanted something in New York where they could demonstrate to their home crowd their ability to wave the magic wand, and what better than the rather run-down Rihga Royal, a fifty-six-storey hotel bang in the middle of Manhattan on 53rd and 7th.

Ceriale, our magic man from Blackstone, is a man who gets very excited and, rather like me, has to share his excitement with others. Immediately. So he was on the phone to Chris about ten seconds after it looked like Blackstone had an option to buy the hotel, and he asked both of us to come over to see the most amazing opportunity God had bestowed since Columbus set sail. Exciting indeed, and we were on our way on a fucking freezing winter's day in 2005.

We arrived at noon and made a McLaren pit stop at the Mandarin Oriental in Columbus Circle, where we were going to stay, before walking over to find the Rihga. We had a quick lunch at *Café Grey* in the AOL Time Warner Center, and thought back on how, in 1999, while the drawings for this massive twin-towered building were still on the back of an envelope, we had held talks with the developers about putting *Pétrus* in there. It had only been after we had had sight of the projected rents that we decided to pull out, and looking around now, it was probably the right decision. It looked like a tough call on those people, like Jean-Georges Vongerichten and Thomas Keller, who had launched restaurants in a building that, at night, resembled an aircraft hangar. They were both seasoned restaurateurs, particularly Jean-Georges, who had already spread himself throughout New York, and Thomas Keller, who had the amazing *French Laundry* on the West Coast. But I still wondered if restaurant guests would mind coming down three floors on an escalator at night when all the shops were closed.

John Ceriale was waiting for us at the Rihga, and I realized as I stepped into the foyer that, once again, this man must be a shit-hot visionary. The place was just plain fucking awful. Originally built as a block of apartments, it had been turned into a hotel and opened just before 9/11. This immediately suggested that there must have been massive compromises in terms of space or, rather, lack of it, when it came to bringing in hotel facilities. After all, if you build a block of flats, you don't think about pantries and house-keeping space on each floor and about kitchens in the bowels of the building to service the guests. Just to really make the place look attractive, next door to the hotel was an Avis rentals depot, but bad as that might be, we then descended into the hellhole of the kitchen. This was grim beyond measure, and we knew at once that the whole place would need to be gutted to a concrete shell. This was going to cost serious bucks, and there was John Ceriale praising this nightmare as though he had discovered Tutankhamun's bank deposit. It was already understood that we would provide the kitchen, while Blackstone did out the hotel and the restaurants. We would be in for at least $2 million, and I wasn't too sure that would be enough. Upstairs in the restaurant, things weren't much better. It was dark and dingy, and no one could find the light switch, not that it mattered much when it was finally found. The place was sad beyond grief-stricken, and once again, it would be a case of ripping out everything in sight and starting with a nice clean sheet of white paper. 'Fuck me, John,' I remember saying, 'are you sure about this?' John just looked through me. 'Gordon, there are times in life when you have to be brave. Have balls, Gordon. Have balls. The French have an expression: *Courage, mon ami.*'

We toured the rest of the hotel with John Ceriale's rose-tinted glasses on, and apart from the dynamic views from the top penthouses, we could see little to give us a hard-on. But, and this is the big word, BUT it was bang in central Manhattan. What with the infectious enthusiasm of the Blackstone boys, we were hooked and ready to run back to London with stories of how we would knock this town for six. The following morning, Chris and I got up early, put on our shorts and T-shirts, and went running around the outer perimeter of Central Park. As we ran, everyone was looking at us as though we were from Planet Wobble, and it suddenly dawned on us that it was minus two degrees, and we were dressed for the South of France in July. We were so fired up that we just didn't notice the cold. That's what happens when you get passionate.

Building the kitchens was down to us. In all fairness, the clearance of the existing pile of excrement was Blackstone's job, and they tackled it with such bravado that we were suddenly given this vast high-rise void with all the tiles ripped out, air-con ducting truncated and that smell of concrete I remembered from *The Connaught* build. Finding kitchen planners and suppliers was not as easy as we thought. We just imagined that such people would be every-where, desperate to supply Gordon Ramsay with a kitchen designed by out-of-work NASA technicians. And where did we discover that *all* kitchen designers come from? In a word, California, which is roughly as far as London is from New York. This means that every time we needed advice, a plan, an estimate, the little fuckers had to come over from LA.

So we got busy with our West Coast friends, designing a kitchen big enough to service a fine dining restaurant with forty-five covers, a restaurant for more relaxed dining that could seat eighty-five, room service for 560 suites, banqueting for over 250 guests, a chef's table and a staff canteen for 250 employees. It was to be a fucking showpiece on a scale that we had never done before. From the design stage, we had to commission a firm to construct the kitchen and another firm to build everything around it. We had to lock into the amputated ducting and service pipework of the hotel, and somehow make it all work. As construction eventually got started, we had a battle with the hotel construction that was going on around us. As the restaurant was being put together, the hotel rooms were being built and the foyer was undergoing major surgery – all at the same time. Meanwhile, the hotel remained open. As someone said, Blackstone never closes down a revenue stream, however much of a nightmare this causes for employees and guests alike.

New York was always going to be a challenge or, to be more precise, a long series of challenges that would test our resolve as much as anything, and having taken the decision to move forward with this project, it just became a matter of how long we could hold our breath under water. As the kitchen construction in New York got under way, there was not much else we could do over there but to enlist the help of someone who knew the New York restaurant market, someone who could point out the pitfalls and describe a path through the jungle of labour law, permits, unions, liquor licences, menu pricing, salary levels, credit terms, banks and one or two million other subjects that needed our attention.

That meant we urgently needed the help of a series of fixers, most of whom could talk the hind legs off a rodeo horse. They flew over to see what we were all about and ate well at our restaurants in order to help orchestrate the opening of *Gordon Ramsay at The London (NYC)*. Over the next few months, most of them completely fooled us into thinking that all our questions were being answered and that New York posed no more problems than opening a deli in Marylebone High Street. We could just never get a straight reply to anything we wanted to know. Each question had to 'be adapted' to the New York way of life, so ask the fixers about salary levels and any ancilliary payments, such as insurance, and they would go off to investigate. That is the sort of information you hold in your head, have at your fingertips, and can recite like a parrot.

If that wasn't bad enough, we ran into trouble with our main man, our general manager, in New York. He was just full of hocus-pocus, and led us to believe that he could negotiate with the unions, source the best employees, navigate his way through all the wages and tipping systems, and run the place for us. He couldn't have tidied up the bean bags in a crèche, if the truth were known. A bad appointment is a disaster because not only do you look like a prick to everyone around who has realized that you have dropped a bollock long before it dawns on you, but it is just so disruptive in that you have to sack him, find a replacement, settle the new person down, and all at a time when your confidence in your interviewing talents is at an all-time low. That's the bummer about interviewing. You never see the person who is going to come and do the job. All you see is the cardboard cut-out in front of you, with the cracks all carefully airbrushed, the tape inserted with the right sound-track, and a whole load of bollocks they know you want to hear.

'How would you deal with staff infidelity?'

'Hey, sir, I would take a very firm hand and get to the bottom of the problem immediately, sir. I would ask all the right questions until I found out, sir, what had happened and take it along the appropriate route, sir. You know, it's very important that I can trust my lieutenants, and I would have a number of tests that would expose inappropriate behaviour at a very early stage, sir.'

You know it is total crap, and that this general manager just happens to hate confrontation. The higher up the position, the more important it is to get it right first time. I am sure that big corporations get it wrong sometimes, but when I hear of the interview processes that go on for days and days, I know that the best way of all is to carefully watch out for people already in the workplace, and then swoop in with a better offer. Just don't do it to your mates, or you won't have any left in about two minutes flat. Staff recruitment is, as sure as eggs is eggs, the key to your success or failure. Get the wrong person to fly the kite and it will never take off, no matter how strong the breeze.

So Chris went over and 'let him go', as they say. Chris has, perhaps unfairly, gained the reputation as the executioner or the Grim Reaper, so that every time he suddenly appears in a restaurant, everyone immediately wonders who is for the chopping board. I also know that he hates doing it, but he will always grab the nettle if it needs doing.

The one thing that was completely new to us involved the unions, of course. Now, however bad or difficult this might be, I could always console myself with the fact that we were no longer faced with having to deal with the Mafia. For some reason, and maybe I have to thank Rudy Giuliani for this, they had gone off, probably to earn a living from another industry. It happens. A career change in mid-life. Who knows? The stories I used to hear of how restaurants were told which laundry to use had filled me with dread. Not that the linen wouldn't have been cleaned properly, but just imagine if we had a cash flow problem or a problem over missing napkins. Who is going to get heavy with that lot? Fucking hell. *The Godfather* put the spooks up me, and that was just a piece of Hollywood, but I know I'm not the one who is going to sleep with the fishes, that's for sure.

Most of the union negotiations had been carried out by Blackstone, but we were beginning to realize the enormity of the salary bills, not because everyone was earning so much, but because of the sheer number of employees that were needed to run a twenty-four-hour operation when staff could only work for seven and a half hours a day. Chris went along to meet the head honcho at Local Six, the seemingly innocuous name of one of the most powerful unions in New York, which just happened to look after our interests. As he said afterwards, he put on his best suit and tie, polished his toecaps and then met this guy who was so immaculate that you just knew he wore matching pants and socks in case a truck ran him over or he got lucky. There were razor-sharp creases in his impeccable suit, his tie had been put on with a micrometer and his wrist sported a Rolex the size of Big Ben. Chris said that he felt like a hobo next to him. Apparently, the building was a tired, grubby place until, of course, you got to the fifth floor up a dedicated elevator, accompanied by some muscleman. Then the doors opened, and there was the Union Palace with Head Honcho's desk roughly the size of Texas, covered with a million framed, glossy photocall pictures of himself with family, friends, governors, senators and probably the Pope somewhere. This was just a diplomatic visit, but somehow, you knew at once that it wasn't you who was in the driving seat. Take it a few months down the line, and there we were, open. The kitchen was humming, the whole hotel was rocking and rolling, and there I was, just walking through the kitchen when the room service phone rang. I looked at it and knew that if Chris or I answered it – in our own kitchen, part of our own restaurant, business, company, demise and territory – there would be fifteen room service staff walking out on the pretext that I was stealing their jobs. It might mean that the guest didn't get his hamburger quite so quickly, but the union is there to protect its members first. Fuck me. How did that situation ever come about?

The days go on, and the building schedule is in tatters. No one quite knows when it is all going to open, but for sure it isn't going to be for July 2006, as everyone had been led to believe. The interior designer is still in creative mode, and we know that half the stuff, which is on twelve- or fourteen-week lead times, hasn't even been ordered. It's a nightmare we always seem to go through. These creative geniuses are holding up our kitchen programme while they decide on a shade of pink for the drawer liner that no one will ever see. Bomb site to building site to construction site: each phase evolves, and gradually, ever so gradually, the place comes together. The trouble is: we have to press the button on staff recruitment, and the timing is all wrong. The builders promise a finished area for staff training on Monday, so everyone turns up on Monday, only to find that Hank the Hammer had discovered some asbestos over the weekend or a conduit that was more structural than anyone had thought, and there is a fortnight's delay. Great, guys. As the spending grew, I had some bad moments of despair. Had I put my head in the noose? Were all those happy fuckers right when they said that I was mad? Despair? Yes, but only passing, and only fleetingly at three in the morning.

As time grows more desperate, the kitchen construction bills rise. Clearly, there is full employment for these people in New York, and they know that you are totally fucking stuffed without their goodwill. We pay more money. They find more problems. And more money … until the kitchen is suddenly looking wonderful. Vast areas of tiling, Whiterock cladding, stainless steel and the beautiful Rorgue stoves from France. They are the first to ever enter the US, and they look fucking amazing. When the stockpots are full and there are thirty chefs busy in their preparations, the place comes alive. It is the biggest kitchen in the world, as far as I'm concerned, and it is going to make us a lot of money. Eventually. The dining room is also beginning to look glamorous, and I think that maybe I was being a bit harsh on the designer. On the other hand, I revisit this opinion when, after we have been open for a month, the locks on the loos still don't work. Over-engineered locks that don't work is just too much for me to understand. What's wrong with a fucking bolt?

The opening thrash is upon us, and New York's finest come for a nose at *The London*. The invitation list has been drawn up carefully by an agency that knows its way around New York society, so as not to upset anyone and certainly not to miss anyone out. I'm nervous as hell, as it's not easy to impress on a first night when there are no tables and chairs in the dining rooms and, moreso, when there is no dinner. The champagne flows. I think of Chris describing New York's skinny lizzies as social X-rays, and I can see why. They are all here, and the magnet is the kitchen, where true theatre is taking place. The society photographers are all over the place, and everybody wants to get a look-in. I venture into the kitchen, and a tight scrum immediately forms around me. I see faces of celebrities that have popped straight out of *Hello!* or *OK!*

For me, fun as though this may be, the important time is tomorrow, when the cash till starts to ring its head off. We need people sitting at the table, eating and drinking, and until we have that, we are not making money. The party clears around 11 p.m., and we then have a crazy night getting everything ready for the morning breakfast service. Before we do that, we break and I take all those who put this together over to Milos in the neighbouring street. Great, simple fish, cooked exactly as you want it and with no more adornment than some olive oil. We are all as high as kites, and feel that the hard work is all behind us.

How stupid can you get?

For some reason, we did something really dumb. We have never really paid much attention to the critics after an opening, but now, in New York, we hold our breath for the arrival of the *New York Times*'s Frank Bruni. Michelin is our barometer of what we stand for in fine dining, and they have always done us proud. Now we are anticipating a good write-up from someone we don't know anything about, except that he is guaranteed to fly against all the hype and PR that has been flooding the media. It is only our vanity that makes us think that we are going to get something good from him. We wait. And we wait. And after he has visited us five times, he awards us two out of four stars.

We are disappointed for nearly ten minutes, and having looked up the standard of other two-star establishments in New York, we get on with it. After all, the restaurant was booked to the rafters for the next two months, and we could console ourselves with the thought that we must be the best two-star restaurant in New York. The one thing that I did pick up and turn over in my mind was the whisper that Gordon Ramsay didn't have a 'wow' factor. This is interesting, because I don't know if we do 'wow' stuff. I think I know what it is, but it's probably just difficult to put on a plate. It's a bit like trying to work out what makes a restaurant work. There is simply no set formula. The rules are broken all the time, and no one knows what is going to be a guaranteed success. Is it not the same when a stage show is launched or a film released?

The wages are high, very high, or in the parlance of green-dollar bills, they add up to around $200,000 a week. It is unbelievable that, in this day and age, everyone in New York gets paid weekly. It's like no one trusts anyone or no one can budget their way through a whole month, so it's drip-fed on a weekly basis. I wonder if President Bush gets his salary paid weekly. It was vital that we immediately got to work on this. If all union employees are paid by the hour, then we have to control how many hours everyone works, and when we don't need their services, we stand them down for that period. The overtime is colossal, and this becomes the focus of our attention, but somehow, the urgency of this does not percolate through to Neil Ferguson, our head chef.

He was our first choice, picked simply because he was one of our very best chefs, having worked with Angela Hartnett at *The Connaught* for the previous three years. The problem was that, in New York, we had a massive food and beverage operation with all sorts of hurdles to jump over, and Neil was simply too nice a man to get brutal when necessary.

Chris pays one of his visits to New York, and Neil steps down with good grace, conceding that he probably isn't the man for New York. Instead, we look to his Number Two, Josh Emmett, the tall, good-looking New Zealander who has spent the past three years running *The Savoy Grill* for us. He has clearly seen which way the wind has been blowing, and he steps in to take over. Within a couple of weeks, the whole economic picture begins to change. The overtime disappears, and the weekly wage bill drops dramatically to around $145,000 a week. Food margins are taken in hand and rattled until we start to see acceptable percentages. This becomes a classic story of how a brilliant chef could only be a chef. Try and broaden his horizon to include management and all the other skills outside of the kitchen, and things go pear-shaped. Neil's departure is 100 per cent our fault. We simply didn't think this through, and luckily, we have a stand-by who will approach the job in a whole new way. We need a chef who can put on armour, as well as whites, and push through tough policies if this operation is to become a successful commercial venture.

All this is happening as we hear the devastating news that Alain Ducasse, who, in my book, is the world's premier chef, is exiting from *Essex House* after five years. Rumour has it that the unions will be moving in if he stays on, and he already knows it is difficult to make money in the present climate. This is a real shame, as his restaurant is very, very good, and I know that Chris, after this news, will be paying it a visit very soon. It is the perfect setting for a recruitment drive.

For many of us, *Essex House* became the best restaurant in New York after what, by all accounts, had been a very shaky start. Alain had launched in New York with horrendously high prices and with scant attention to the press. In return, they had written stories of the craziness of the French, who offered sixteen different types of water at the start of dinner and a cushion of ten pens when it came to signing the bill. Also, there were little stools at the side of each table for the ladies to put their handbags. All too much for New Yorkers, and they belted him. It took two years before he recovered and the city forgave him.

The hotel is eventually complete. Only half the floors are open at the outset, which is probably just as well, since we have to ease ourselves gently into the disciplines of room service. There will be over 560 suites by the time the penthouses are finished, and we are taking a radical approach to food delivery. There is no room for big trolleys, so we have installed in every suite a beautiful round table that looks like a coffee table until you spin the top around to adjust the level, and, *voilà*, it becomes a dining table.

Outside, dinner has arrived in a hot box and the room service waiter sets the table and delivers each course in sequence. No trolley is wheeled in, with the whole shooting match all at once. The response from our guests is good, and out of the blue, Mr Bruni does a piece on the best ten room service operations in Manhattan's high-end hotels. Who comes out top but The London! Fantastic.

When I got the opportunity to escape from *The London* for a brief walk around, I would take in what there is to see in the neighbouring streets. The Whole Foods store beneath the AOL Center is fascinating, particularly at lunch, when the queues are 100 deep. Organic food is clearly a favoured option in the US these days, and as I walked around, I wondered how the hell they deal with out-of-date produce. There are simply acres and acres of everything that is good to eat, all beautifully presented, but you would need an invasion of a million food-deprived, retreating foot soldiers to make any impression on their stock levels. One floor above is Williams-Sonoma, which is elegant and probably horribly expensive. I saw kitchen ware that had been given beautiful colours, interesting designs and chic touches to seduce the homemaker, and from the chef's point of view, it is all toffee, as the pots and pans do exactly the same as their counterparts in the commercial kitchen. Having said that, I thought about launching a similar store in London, with the big demo kitchen to lure people in, and I got that tingle that comes when an exciting, sexy commercial idea raises the adrenaline levels.

I like visiting other restaurants, and *Per Se* is one of my favourites, in spite of its location at the top of the AOL Center. I have had some very good courses there, and the kitchen is beautiful to see. It is very different to our fine-dining offering in *The London*, and I wonder if they find it as hard to make money in New York as we do. This building is also the home of The Mandarin Oriental, where I have stayed a few times, but it's not really for me. The whole business of modern hotels perched on top of office buildings invariably means a change of lift somewhere on the way up, so my favourite retreat has become Nick Jones's Soho House. It's a bit off the beaten track, but travelling in Manhattan is fun, anyway.

Being a chef is not helpful when it comes to foreign exchange. I know what happens, and I can deal with it, but I have no idea why it happens. How is it that Big America has such a weak dollar, and this tiny little country here has a pound that is stronger than a bulldozer? It never used to be like that, but I am all in favour of it while we are constructing kitchens in New York and the pound stretches out towards the horizon. It's just that, when the capital expenditure has been paid off, the whole money exchange goes the other way, and everything we earn is worth half as much. So, unless you buy property in the US and use it there, there isn't, strictly speaking, any point in making money in America. The same is true round the world, in Australia and South Africa, where there are numerous opportunities but weak currencies.

In the middle of all this, we had a disaster in London involving the payment of airline tickets. After we had closed our restaurant in Glasgow, airline ticketing didn't happen very often. Trips to Dubai and Tokyo were invariably paid for by Hilton as part of our deal with them, and they dealt with the purchasing of the tickets. If I was off to Singapore to do work with the airline, then, of course, they paid for my travelling. But suddenly there was a need for research into the cheapest way to fly, whether it be in economy or business class, and suddenly we were sending over staff to New York by the planeload. Also, of course, both Chris and I were travelling all over the place to look at possible projects, and Chris used a contact he had known for over ten years. His name was Ted. It always worked well, as Ted was efficient and always managed to get exactly what we wanted in terms of limos to pick us up for the airport or freebie tickets on Eurostar. Tickets were paid for prior to a flight, and everyone was content with this arrangement. It soon became apparent that there was a need for a travel manager, and Ted offered to take on this responsibility. So he started full-time at the office, and every time we needed travel itineraries, Ted did the business.

One day, my financial director came up to me with a statement showing something like £60,000 owing to a travel agent. Detailed were the names of our staff, together with some names that were not familiar. I passed it on to Chris, who said that he would query it with Ted, which he did, and Ted promised to sort it out. Then one morning,

Ted came in to see Gillian and told her he might have a problem with regard to his personal finances. So upset was he that Gillian immediately sent him home and dropped by Chris's office to mention this rather unlikely turn of events. After that, she went down to Ted's office, which was situated in the bowels of the building, and opened his filing cabinet. Inside were piles of invoices, statements and warning letters, in no order, but as though they had just been thrown in there. On later examination, there appeared to be six travel agents who had submitted invoices and clearly hadn't been paid. The outstanding total was around £350,000, accumulated in about three months. What a fucking bombshell.

A closer look revealed that Ted had been using Gordon Ramsay Holdings as a travel agent, and had been booking tickets for all his clients, as well as our own staff. The balloon went up, and suddenly there were all these people chasing us for money. In fact, they had been chasing their money for weeks, but somehow Ted had managed to divert all the relevant mail to himself and make a thousand empty promises. Among all the pieces of mail were at least three writs, all in the name of Gordon Ramsay Holdings. Great PR if that had ever gotten out. A phone call to each of the travel agents explained the situation, and, in the main, they were understanding, but it didn't stop their claims. So now we were facing six separate legal battles, all with slightly different circumstances and each with substantial legal bills. This was about what should have been nothing more than a side expense, but while we were so busy setting up New York, we managed to miss what could turn out to be one very big, costly mistake. Lessons to be learned? Put in systems that allow you to check and check again. Here was a situation where the prepayment of flights by cheque changed to credit-card payments because there was less and less time for booking. So accounts thought that all the flights were being paid for by credit cards, and the credit-card holders imagined that cheques were being sent. A further complication was that Ted had 'sold' batches of ten business-class tickets for £19,000 to us, and we had had to pay for them on the nail. This gave a really worthwhile saving on tickets that would probably cost in excess of £4,000 each. Except, of course, that these special deals never existed, and when we came to use the tickets, Ted simply ordered them from one of our six friendly travel agents, who all thought they were dealing with Gordon Ramsay Holdings and what a great new account they had. When their bills turned up for flights that we had already 'paid for', their charges were at the full rate and, yes, we used them and will be required to pay for them. Fuck, fuck, fuck.

In trying to slow down the costs involved in New York while we waited for the turnover to grow, the two gladiators in the circus were Gillian Thomson in London and an amazing find called Edna Cunningham. Between them, they pummelled the weak and praised the strong until, gradually, the picture began to change in our favour. Blackstone, who had been less than accurate in their forecasting of completion dates, realized that we were being penalized because of this while staff were just hanging around, and they held back from starting the rent until all the revenue streams were operating.

The public-relations firm we brought in was the Susan Magrino Agency. They are on home territory in New York, and although we took a while to get used to the New York way of doing things, we soon got the hang of it. Funny business, PR. It has no real method of measurement, and even if your agency is amazingly good at getting you in the journals and the newspaper columns, you still don't really know if the level of bookings is a direct result of this or not. Bad restaurants advertise, good restaurants get talked about, and that is why we can never consider dispensing with the agency fees when the going gets rough.

New York had become a lesson about getting the right people for the job. Before, in our earlier ventures, staff just came along at the right time and proved their worth. This city presented us with a much bigger challenge, and we had been far too happy to accept what was presented to us without checking and monitoring all the time. It was an expensive lesson, but it didn't bring us to our knees, and it never will. But we shall be more fucking on the ball in future.

It has been a long, hard fight to get to where we are in New York. In London we have been spoiled rotten, and with few exceptions, all our restaurants have done well, virtually from their starts, with little of the street fighting that we have experienced across the pond. New York has eaten away at our London operational resources and approximately $10 million in hard cash. Will it succeed? Too fucking right it will succeed, despite the piranha press trying to consume me, the voracious unions, and the general reluctance to acknowledge that we are good. We are there to stay, and while we are learning how to be American on the East Coast, we shall be opening up in LA by the end of 2007.

CHAPTER EIGHTEEN

A HELPING HAND

*The charity industry can teach you a
great deal about business in its
use of limited resources, and
the need for motivation
for those in charge.*

ABOUT A MONTH ago, a letter arrived at our head office
addressed to 'Tana Ramsey' *[sic]*. It was handwritten on
both sides of the paper, and extended to several pages, as
it detailed the life this woman had led with her husband and
their six children. They were always short of money and
lived in very limited accommodation, but nevertheless, they
were anxious to foster children to add to their family. She
went on to say that she had followed the press reports and
pictures of our family, and felt very comfortable in detail-
ing her own situation, as she knew that Tana would understand that what she was about to ask for would make life
a great deal easier. They had found the perfect house that
would accommodate everyone, and it was on the market
for £850,000, and, she went on, would Tana be able to
forward the funds as quickly as possible, as she didn't want
to lose the house?

Fortunately, charity requests rarely take this head-on approach. For famous people, or those with deeper pockets, the charity request is an everyday occurrence. For me, it's about 100 requests every day, with appeals pouring through the letterboxes of Gordon Ramsay Holdings, its restaurants or my front door at home. I imagine that everyone gets asked for charity in one form or another, but that is for hard cash, whereas for me, that's hardly ever the case. Everyone wants my time, my restaurant tables, signed books or recipes. Hardly anyone asks me for money, which is interesting. It suggests that charity organizers see me as a way of generating charity funds, rather than just writing a cheque. They plan their fundraising activities to include a raffle with a table for two at *Gordon Ramsay at Claridge's*, a signed book or anything that will entice people to buy raffle tickets. It's very much with the thought that nothing is for free, and although people have warm hearts, they do not take to the idea of just giving money. Give them a rock concert or a chance of winning a holiday in Mauritius, and you'll get an immediate response.

Charity requests, like all the mail, are dealt with in the office of Gordon Ramsay Holdings by a full-time assistant. There are some very definite rules that we have had to come up with to deal with this side of our business. The most important is that every request gets a reply, irrespective of whether the answer is a 'yes' or a 'no'. Somebody is trying to raise funds, and that is, without doubt, a fucking hard, often unrewarding job. No reply will suggest that the request has been binned, and that is hardly going to encourage anyone to keep up the good fight.

How do you start to decide who or what is a deserving cause? That is a nightmare made easier by some simple disqualifying conditions. They may sound arrogant and discriminating, but you have somehow got to find a way through to a shortlist. So any letter starting, 'Dear Mr Ramsey' gets a 'no'. If you can't be bothered to spell my name right, then you are hardly going to endear yourself to your target. The same is true for 'Dear Sir or Madam', 'Dear Manager' or 'Hi'. They are not going to make the cut either. Five pages of a closely typed explanation building up to the request will die early, along with the reader's patience, and letters that arrive without a stamp smack of carelessness. The biggest decider, of course, assuming that you have battled through the preliminaries, is the beneficiary of the request. And here it becomes very subjective. Animal charities haven't got a look-in – not because I don't like cats and dogs or even the occasional donkey, but because I just get the impression that they are already looked after better than any other worthy cause, and I always wonder why the RSPCA is 'Royal' and the NSPCC is just plain 'National'. Schools, or at least the parents of children at school, are forever asking for help to buy computers or gym equipment, and I guess that this should be the responsibility of the school budgeting committee. Moreso if it's a private school, where the parents surely carry the responsibility to finance the school's requirements. I am not saying that they shouldn't be asking. I just don't feel responsive to these requests.

I have been running marathons for some years now, and perhaps that is what stimulates so many requests for me to sponsor people who want to do the maddest sporting challenges for their chosen charities. The request frequently comes from someone who has had a cancer scare or lost a relative or friend, and just wants to thank the local hospital for what they did. There is always excitement in the request as the letter explains to me exactly which mountain is to be climbed on the back of a yak or where the river runs, which is about to be navigated in a kitchen sink. I'm afraid that these letters end up in the 'no' tray. I once met Chris Moon, a totally selfless man who hooked up with Chris some years ago on a Sahara marathon. Now there is an inspiration, someone who has become the most amazing fundraiser. He had been working for the Halo Trust, teaching people how to disarm anti-personnel mines, when one went off. He lost an arm and much of one leg, and when he had recovered, he set about raising money for charity. Chris took him over to South Africa to run the 56-mile Comrades race one year, and because of Chris Moon's celebrity status as a charity fundraiser extraordinaire, the two of them were allowed in the elite start. When asked by one of the other runners how he got into the starting pen, Chris Moon just looked up and said, 'Fucking hell, it was expensive. It cost me an arm and a leg.' So yaks, kitchen sinks and all the other ways of transporting yourself over difficult terrain really pass me by after meeting the one-legged, one-armed master of money-raising in the sports arena.

I am also not very keen on responding to people who forget to mention which charity they are hoping I will support. 'Dear Mr Ramsay, We think that the Chef's Table at *Pétrus* would be just the right prize in our raffle and will undoubtedly be a major attraction in our charity draw. We shall, of course, include an acknowledgement in our programme.' That's all I'm told. It could be for giving holidays to tired tax inspectors or providing retirement homes for food critics. No shortlist for you, my friend.

I don't help the bigger charities. They undoubtedly do great work, but I just see too many requests from them, and I am always wondering how much money actually gets through to the cause. Don't get me wrong on this. I do understand that successful charities need professional administrators and that they have to be paid, but I prefer to know that the bulk of donations goes to the cause. For instance, I like StreetSmart, the charity that persuades us to put a £1 surcharge on every table we serve through November and December. They have sponsors who pay for all the administration separately, so that the total of the raised funds goes directly to the homeless. How can you fault that? You get the impression that a lot of thought has been put into this charity and the way it works. It raises large sums of money without having to ask countless people for donations. The hardest part for those running StreetSmart is persuading restaurants to take on the scheme.

Once that has been achieved, the process of fundraising is relatively painless. It reminds me of how a well-known children's charity used to persuade factory workers to donate 1p from their monthly salaries. No one could ever complain about the amount, and in big workforces, it soon mounted up. Even in hard times, no one was ever going to cancel this arrangement unless they objected on principle.

If it sounds as though there is no one left to qualify for the shortlist, then be assured that that is not the case. There are a thousand good causes, usually directed at children and hospice care, that tug at the heartstrings, but that is another subject in itself.

Sometimes, the best way of bringing real help is to replace charity with what has become widely labelled as 'tough love'. Invariably, this is a method of last resort, and comes after all the usual routes of help, care and love have been travelled. If ever there was a case of charity beginning at home, it has been with my mother, in her countless attempts to get my brother, Ronnie, clean. He has been a drug addict for so many years that I have lost count, and there have been so many occasions when we have all thought that he was going to make it. I have provided money to pay for clinics, new teeth, training courses and employment, while the whole family provided love, care and encouragement, yet it all seemed to do little but land him in a Balinese jail for drug possession. There comes a point when there is nothing left to give and nothing left to try. The only way forward is to withdraw help and charity, and let him sink or swim. This is tough love indeed, and it provides an insight into the complexities of charity. Money, love and being there for someone are all elements of help, but you need to understand how people are affected by them. Put simply, if my brother wants money from me nowadays, then it is highly likely that it is to pay for the drugs that he craves. To give it to him will help no one. To say no creates a tension that will obliterate any other form of help, such as encouraging him to keep to a healthy diet or get a job. To walk away at that point is probably the only course, and you have to hope that he will come to his senses.

Drug-related charity is, invariably, a catalogue of disappointment and uncertainty, going by my experiences with my brother. Fortunately, however, you are sometimes privileged to see a truly positive side of charity. Three years ago, I was approached by an amazing woman, Dr Margo Whitefield, whom I had met at the start of the 2002 Great North Run. There was I, all ready to run, not sure if I was fit enough, and there was Margo in a wheelchair, eager for the starter's gun. She wrote to me some time after the race to ask if I would become the patron of the Scottish Spina Bifida Association. To be honest, I didn't understand what spina bifida was until she patiently described the condition and how the charity worked to improve the lives of children and adults who suffer from it. I was overwhelmed by her approach, and immediately agreed to become involved. Later I met Deborah Roe, the fundraising and events manager, who took me under her wing and, in the following years, guided me through their programmes and events for raising funds. In 2005, they opened their new family support centre and head office after a highly effective 'Buy a Brick' campaign, and I visited them and met some of the children who suffer from the disorder.

Talk about bringing you down to earth. I was knocked out by how these children just carried on with their lives, even with such severe disabilities. It was an immensely moving experience. Here were young people who dealt daily with what I would have regarded as climbing a mountain, and it was an experience that I shall never forget. It was truly humbling, and this year I shall make sure that I take Tana with me to meet everyone. The other impressive aspect was the extraordinary passion and single-mindedness of those who run the organization. The motivational drive is there for all to see, and no wonder people like Deborah Roe achieve so much. The staff clearly care deeply about the cause, and I wonder if this driving force is just compassion, or whether or not there is anger that such tragedies can occur. Whatever, the determination to succeed has a strength that is rarely seen in commercial management, where staff are fully preoccupied with the size of their pay packets and the chances of promotion. Stimulation is an important part of your job, and any manager who is not aware of this should definitely not be managing anyone.

I see street beggars in almost every city and large town that I visit. They don't surprise me any more, but I often wonder if they have adopted this way of life because they are lazy, have had some sort of breakdown, or make too much money out of it to bother looking for a more regular lifestyle. Some beggars are funny and have a charm that is honed to extract the fiver from your pocket. I can become very judgemental when I see someone asking for 'your loose change, guv'nor' while they are drawing heavily on a fag. If they expect me to support their habit, they can think again. Bag ladies are rare, but extremely difficult to ignore. Do I imagine that this is the way Mum could have gone if she had not been able to deal with Dad, or do we just feel that, for some reason, women should not be in this situation? There was a time when I would find some coins in my pocket for a beggar, and then I started to think about it. Why am I doing it? Is it just to ease my embarrassment at being asked? Is it to ease my conscience? Or do I think it might really help? The answer was simply that it made the moment go away, and maybe that's the beggar's weapon. It's almost intimidation, except it's yourself and your reactions that you are afraid of. One thing is for sure. It wasn't going to alter his life. The only thing that would have done that is if he had asked me for a job in the kitchens. When I see someone selling the *Big Issue*, I have no problem buying a copy. It is a brilliant idea, and you can invariably see motivation and energy in the vendor. Self-respect has been restored, and they are back, working their way up the ladder.

Charity has become a huge industry in its own right. It is part of our social fabric, and clearly has a highly important role to play. For someone like myself who is asked to help on a daily basis, it means that I have to focus on the few areas where I can help best. I have already learned not to reach in my pocket every time a good cause is put in front of me. Too often, this just doesn't achieve the right result. There has to be self-respect where charitable handouts are concerned, and if it's likely that respect will fall by the wayside for whatever reason, then it's probably best that I don't contribute. There has to be some sort of plan, which means no more than concentrating my efforts on causes that I feel strongly about. Seeing what children with spina bifida are faced with and how they cope is an inspiration that makes me want to be involved and supportive. A helping hand is there for these children because they need it to help themselves. They have self-respect in bucketfuls, and that is how it should be.

CHAPTER NINETEEN

HOLLYWOOD CALLS

Meeting people with foresight and putting
your trust in them is a scary prospect, but
sometimes you have to listen to your
instincts and trust people.

2004 WAS STILL early days for me in television. *Kitchen Nightmares* had kicked off with some good audience ratings, and I had just completed *Hell's Kitchen* for ITV. This had squeezed through well, too, but it wasn't something I felt comfortable with, particularly when it involved celebrities who had their own agendas. Looking back, *Hell's Kitchen* was a series of near misses, of on-screen conflicts that left the production team wondering what to do the following night. There was no settled script, which left the whole show open to a spontaneity that was unsettling. To be fair, it was the first attempt at something like this, where two teams of minor celebrities were encouraged to compete in preparing dinner for an invited audience each night. They were, of course, fucking useless, and were far more interested in appearing as celebrated individuals with their hissy fits, tears, breakdowns and anything that might make good headlines in the red tops the following morning. In that format, it just wasn't for me, and when the US arm of Granada showed an interest in the format of the programme, I was less than enthusiastic. Having said that, I was curious enough to get on a plane with Chris and visit Los Angeles.

It wasn't just LA that we were heading for, but Hollywood. Holy fuck! Gordon Ramsay goes to Hollywood. Even Mum smiled about that. We stayed at the hip, if not slightly weird, Chateau Marmont, and were driven everywhere in a black Hummer chauffeured by the biggest guy I have ever seen. I mean: muscle big. Chris and I had two of the producers from the UK *Hell's Kitchen* team in tow, and the tight time schedule ensured that we were all on our way to the Fox studios within an hour of arriving. The meeting was with Fox's Mike Darnell, who, we were told, was often credited as the originator of reality TV. Whether it was his exalted position or just because he got up late, he kept us waiting for nearly two hours before arriving with his entourage.

From the moment he entered the room, you would have thought we had been best buddies for years. He is tiny, and it takes a while to get used to this and to his extraordinary energy. He couldn't keep still. Mike explained that he had seen all the episodes of ITV's *Hell's Kitchen* and, although he loved the format, he realized that, if it were to be made for US television, a different approach would be needed. In the States, they don't do B- and C-list celebrities. You are either an A-list celebrity or no one at all. What Mike had in mind was *Hell's Kitchen* with teams made up of real chefs, and at the end, the prize for the winner would be a restaurant. The big question, of course, was how Fox would deal with the inevitable swearing that had become part of the format. Don't imagine that it's all affected. Try standing in a kitchen that's under pressure with fuckwits standing over a dish of incinerated lamb because they had been too busy sulking. Then try talking evenly to them. There may be a St Peter or St Paul somewhere, but certainly not in my kitchen.

The fees for *Hell's Kitchen UK* had been high, but suddenly we were looking at a six-figure sum, which seemed reasonably attractive until I realized they were talking of a fee per episode and that there would be a minimum of ten episodes. So, we were no longer in six, but seven figures. This was extraordinary, as, quite clearly, Fox would be taking a massive chance with a new, untried format and with me, someone no one in the US had ever heard of. The contract would contain an option for five seasons, so if the show was anything like a success, I would be returning for some time to come.

In a way, it was taken for granted that the whole proposal would be moving forward. We were suddenly whizzing around meeting the Arthur Smith team, who would be the programme makers, and then visiting sprawling, empty buildings with huge car lots that were being considered as possible locations. Invariably, they were buildings full of the previous tenants' junk, and looked as though they would take a year to clear out before any construction work could begin. But then, I didn't know how programme makers can make things happen when they get the green light.

We returned home slightly breathless. Not only had I made the decision to turn our backs on any more *Hell's Kitchen* shows in the UK and to move to the more lucrative Channel 4, where I would be making shows I felt happier with, but it seemed that we could still have the benefit of a US presence.

I signed the deal with Fox before Christmas and waited with some trepidation for the following February, 2005, when filming would start. There was plenty of work that needed doing in the meantime, particularly regarding the menus that had to be prepared and tested for the ten shows. I also had to decide whom, from my front-of-house teams, I would take over with me to help organize the restaurant staff. I eventually chose Jean-Philippe Susilovic, who had worked with me since the *Aubergine* days and who was to become a permanent fixture during the following years of *Hell's Kitchen USA*.

The Fox deal was very significant in commercial terms. These were the days before we had really done anything on that side of the pond, with the exception of a few showings of *Kitchen Nightmares* on BBC America and the publication of *A Chef for All Seasons*. This was well before my restaurant in New York had opened, although we were already looking at the US market and working out how best to tackle it. It is a huge market that could offer up revenue streams that would make everything we had done earlier seem like small beer. What we now saw with *Hell's Kitchen USA* was that it supplied the key to unlock the door, and what better key than television?

When I turned up at the end of January in preparation for shooting *Hell's Kitchen*, I couldn't believe what I saw. The rambling lot that I had seen on my first visit had changed beyond recognition. Out of a dump had risen this beautiful restaurant with two open kitchens side by side. It was staggering, even by American standards, that this transformation had taken place. Of course, in addition to the restaurant, there was an immense studio with static cameras placed throughout the restaurant and the kitchens, all linked to the viewing gallery with a wall of screens that would make Houston look small-time. And above this building, on a hoarding the size of a house, was me, dressed as the Devil in hell, surrounded by fire. Fuck me. Just plain amazing. Here was a broadcaster who was not only willing to take a chance on my screen abilities, but was happy to devote a huge budget to my promotion. From my standpoint, you cannot buy that. You can only stand humbly by and hope to fuck that it works and the American public grabs it.

The filming of what turned out to be eleven episodes took the best part of a month. It was hard, but I was in the company of real professionals who had all the ideas and, seemingly, deep pockets. Everyone, from the film crews to wardrobe, was amazingly dedicated. There was an intensity of effort and concentration that fed into the show and reminded me of my kitchens during service. Everyone had a clear of idea of what they had to do, and there were no collisions or duplications of work. It was also a different experience working with contestants who saw the opportunity to land themselves a restaurant with all the attendant publicity. They behaved well, almost without exception, and without all the histrionics that I experienced earlier in London. Having said that, as one or two of the contestants were voted out of the show, things sometimes got a bit fraught, and on at least one occasion, punches were thrown before security could get there. It gave me a chance to see how lawyers can appear from nowhere in the middle of a weekend, totally prepared to launch full-scale litigation. Me? I just kept my head down and got on with making the television show.

By the end of February, the eleven episodes were in the can, and it was just a matter of waiting for Fox to broadcast the opening episodes to see if this show was going to touch America. I had heard all the horror stories of how, in American television, the opening episodes determined the show's future and that, if the ratings were weak, the broadcaster simply pulled the plug and the series died on the spot, standing with its pants down. Fuck knows what it must have been like for Mike Darnell, who had put his head on the chopping block. Plenty of Brits had braved the US screen, only to return with their tails between their legs. It is a fact of life that there is no guarantee that what might work brilliantly in the UK will do the same in the US. Think Mars bars and Hershey bars. They only work in their own backyards. Occasionally, the likes of *Pop Idol* come along and, with a few tweaks, they are successfully groomed for our American cousins, but who knows what they will think about me dressed up as the Devil?

In the meantime, my publisher, Quadrille, was running around getting excited at the prospect of a real American presence. But, in truth, we were all waiting to see what happened. I was in New York the week before the series started to run, and I was just walking down Fifth Avenue when, suddenly, a bus came roaring around the corner, and as I stepped back to make sure it didn't run over my size-fifteens, I suddenly realized that I was staring at myself. The whole fucking side of the bus was an advertisement for Fox's *Hell's Kitchen*, and we were over 3,000 miles from LA. I don't remember anyone asking for copy approval, but what the fuck? How would anyone have predicted a year ago that I would be sailing down Fifth Avenue on the side of a bus?

The show kicked off, and straight away, it was hailed a success. Every week I would receive the viewing figures, and whereas I had hoped to see just one figure representing half of the US, there were pages of these numbers classed in terms of age and demography (I had to look that one up) and percentages compared to other broadcasters. I gave up trying to track it all and just waited to hear if Arthur Smith and Mike Darnell were happy. They were, and within weeks of the show finishing, Fox had informed me that they would be taking up the second-year option. Americans are an insular race and keep themselves to themselves, except, of course, if their president feels that there is a war option somewhere. Apart from the occasional mention in London by a restaurant guest who had seen one of the episodes, the only other way we would have known that somebody somewhere had actually watched *Hell's Kitchen* was when guests recognized Jean-Philippe. He had excelled himself during filming and, no doubt, loved the publicity. Some time later, the silly sod somehow managed to fall from the window of his apartment in south-east London and plunged 55 feet onto solid concrete. Amazingly, he survived, and Chris, who had fielded the call at work on a Sunday morning from Lambeth Council's missing persons office, had to go straight down to King's College Hospital to pick up the pieces. J-P had broken almost every bone in his body and was on life support. Chris had to get hold of his sister and parents in Belgium, who must have suffered a terrible shock. Two weeks later, this bionic man, who had failed to defy gravity, was sitting up in bed and on the mend. The only problem was that his eyes were crossed, and it was a further two weeks before he could see straight.

The final act of my first season of *Hell's Kitchen USA* took place as soon as Chris sent off the invoice. Back came a cheque, minus a 38 per cent deduction by the American Internal Revenue Service on behalf of HMR&C. I never realized that they were such great mates. No doubt, another 2 per cent will be docked in due course.

The following year, we did the second series. It was bigger and better, and clearly the budget had been extended. Everyone was much more relaxed than before, with the confidence built on the previous year's ratings. Whether or not the show had the legs to go the full five years was doubtful, but right now we needed to see how the American public would take to a second series. There were more off-set challenges for the contestants, which gave greater breadth to each programme. On this occasion, the winner would get to take charge of a restaurant in a new resort hotel in Las Vegas.

It was during this second series that ITV tried to woo me again, knowing that, in eighteen months, my contract with Channel 4 would be coming to an end. The head of Granada US was coming back to London to take up the post of head of entertainment at ITV, and he clearly fancied his chances of bringing me along. This was unlikely to ever happen, as I was enjoying what I was doing with Channel 4, and, as described earlier, they came in with a new offer that reflected the value I added to their output. Also, I worked well with Pat Llewellyn, the boss of Optomen TV, the programme makers for *Kitchen Nightmares* and the new *F Word* show. She is a supreme producer when it involves food, and judging by the success of *Kitchen Nightmares*, she had developed a new ability to handle television drama. What better setting for drama than someone's dying restaurant? Added to this, Chris was not particularly keen on the departing Granada US head, and I didn't think any love would be lost there.

Again, *Hell's Kitchen* seemed to appeal to US audiences, and once again, Fox served notice to exercise their option for a third series. This time, it was with a difference. Fox felt that they could expand the Ramsay brand, and they were looking closely at Optomen's *Kitchen Nightmares*. Could it be tweaked to appeal to US audiences? This could be a big problem, as it would highlight the biggest problem for me by that time, which was a complete logjam in the diary. The answer lay with the new head of Granada US, David Gyngell. An Australian with an impressive career in television, he swept in with an energy and drive that immediately appealed to me. He had been over to see Chris, and we both felt that here was a man we could work with and trust with my future in US television. His proposal was to complete the third series of *Hell's Kitchen* and move straight on to making eight episodes of *Kitchen Nightmares*. In the UK, each episode of *Kitchen Nightmares* could take a total of ten days to make, including the filming, travelling and voice-overs, with two days for a revisit later. A business plan would be put in place, and there would be time for the owners to pull through or disappear into obscurity. Some of the restaurants responded magnificently, and others were just shown to be in the wrong business. Either way, there were all the elements of me as the restaurant doctor, administering to the sick and hoping that the patient would recover. If we worked that way in the US and added the thirty days of filming for *Hell's Kitchen*, I would be filming for over four fucking months. To save the situation, David suggested we film each episode in just three days, with different producers and crews at each location so that everything would be ready for me when I arrived on Day One. This was giddy stuff, and would mean fifty-five days straight-off, with no breaks and no gaps, but it was workable. And, again, there would be a six-figure sum for each episode. Because Chris moaned about me having to cut my January holiday short, they 'fully understood' and threw in a further $250,000.

With this huge hurdle cleared, Chris also held out for a shorter contract. Fox's contracts were always for five seasons, and this would extend my commitment to Fox for a further two years past the expiry of the *Hell's Kitchen* contract. If *Hell's Kitchen* sustained its popularity and *Kitchen Nightmares* took off, my 'stock', as Chris put it, would increase considerably and help negotiations for future commissions with Fox or any of the other networks. At first, Fox would not budge an inch, and we turned our backs, as though to walk away. David Gyngell wasn't happy, but understood the situation, and all the preparations came to a halt in a second. Pat Llewellyn, whose company, Optomen, owned the format, was to become one of the executive producers, so, no doubt, she was disappointed. Nevertheless, we all had plenty on our plates, and maybe this wasn't such a bad thing. The timetable would have been manic, and although there were fresh production units for each of the restaurants that we would have visited, I would have had to go straight through, getting to know each director, the set and the 'players' for only three days before moving on and starting all over again. 'What sort of programme would come out of that?' I wondered.

At the last moment, Fox relented and accepted that the *Kitchen Nightmares* contract would extend to three years only, ending at the same time as *Hell's Kitchen*. Fuck, fuck, fuck. They really did want me, because, according to Granada US, they never issued contracts for less than five years. Suddenly, there was uproar as the whole operation sprung to life. There wouldn't be a spare minute in the day, and David would have to put together a detailed itinerary that left no room for error. For me, it was just a matter of telling Tana that our holiday was going to be cut short and that I could see little prospect of making up for it in what was going to be my busiest year yet. How come I always get the crap jobs? Why can't Chris deal with this for me? When I tried to ask him that, he just raised an eyebrow and turned around. There are limits to anything, I guess.

We romped through *Hell's Kitchen* like the first half of a marathon. We had done it all before, and there was, once again, a much-needed increase in the budget to pay for all the helicopters and the extraordinary challenges devised by Arthur Smith and his team. Within thirty days, it was all filmed and ready for the editing suites, while I turned my attention to the very first episode of *Kitchen Nightmares USA*.

By the end of the first three days, I had realized that Fox had a very different take on Pat's format. The idea behind their programme was a story of a bad, bad restaurant with a totally useless, incompetent owner running a broken-down kitchen with no customers. Three days later, everyone had been to hell and back, and there we were: a makeover for the restaurant, heavy neurosurgery on the owner, a revitalized kitchen brigade and customers flooding through the door. It was a thoroughly spellbinding piece of magic with a feel-good factor several layers deep and a fairy-tale ending. Classic American programme making.

The other episodes followed, and although there was not much time for sleep, the motivation and drive that each episode offered abolished any thought of sitting down for a mid-afternoon nap. Added to that, it was fucking cold everywhere.

So it went on until we finally wrapped on the eighth and last of the series. Knackered, I climbed aboard a Virgin Atlantic 777 and made my way back to see how the home fires were burning.

One thing that was becoming clearer all the time was that the US was a very large place, and that, with this physical size, came a large population. Undoubtedly, television was the fast track to recognition, but with a million channels, it was unlikely that everyone was going to be viewing *Hell's Kitchen* at the same time. By now, I had a growing commercial operation with my restaurant at The London in New York, the restaurant in Boca Raton in Florida, and soon there would be the opening of *The Bel Age* in LA, once remodelling of that pink palace was completed. There were also other projects on the drawing board, yet I knew that these areas of activity were not particularly affected by my television profile. The same would be true of publishing, where selling cookbooks was a hard slog in a country that already had its favourite chefs and homemakers. It looked as though I needed to concentrate on programme-making and keeping my commercial restaurant interests under close review. The growth and success would come, but only in time, and provided I kept at it relentlessly.

The third series of *Hell's Kitchen* seemed to reach the sky in its ratings, and suddenly I had Fox asking me to come back and film Series Four and Five before the end of 2007. This would effectively end the contract, and I guess you want every agreement to end on a high note to prepare the ground for future negotiations. It was great to know that *Hell's Kitchen* had produced the ratings that the likes of Mike Darnell had predicted so accurately. I had put my trust in his judgement, just as I had done years before with John Ceriale of Blackstone, and they had put their trust in me to perform.

America was proving a good friend to me, and now I waited to see how *Kitchen Nightmares* would fare.

Both John Ceriale and Mike Darnell imagined projects that I could do, which I had never begun to imagine myself. You can't trust everyone – if you do, you kind of deserve to get fucked. But at the same time, when you run across one of these visionary people with a track record, you sometimes just have to trust them and run with it. That was the lesson of Hollywood for me, and it has worked – so far.

CHAPTER TWENTY

A CHANGE IN
SPENDING HABITS

*One thing to remember about money is that
it comes, you pay your taxes, and it goes.
Only the really big money stays around.*

TALKING ABOUT MONEY is probably as near as I ever get to
what I understand of the term 'philosophy'. When you
haven't got any money, the only thing that you think about
is how more money could change your life. I am sure that
relatively few people seriously set about making more
money, other than by one of the three big hopes: a promotion at work, a lottery win or the untimely death of a benevo-
lent relative. Increasingly, people just steal the stuff.

I never set out to make more money. I really wish I could
say otherwise, but it just hasn't been the case. I have met
people who have made a fortune with intent, and they are
few and far between. Invariably, they are wealthier than I
could ever imagine being because they have become good
at what they set out to do, and that has been their only goal
in life. I can't imagine that Sir Philip Green or the Amstrad
guy just came across it. They were born into the money-

making slot of life, just as royalty wakes up royal or a natural born leader gets lots of pips on his shoulder.

But it is the spending or squirrelling away of money that is the interesting or, to put it more grandly, the 'philosophical' aspect that intrigues me. I was born with zilch, and when money comes about, the question, first of all, is whether or not you are a mean fuck, or do you blow it as though it were water from the kitchen tap? This question is all about you, your genes and what has affected you as you grew up. It's not about the people around you – it's about your reaction to the people around you and how you want them to react towards you and your newly acquired wealth. If you are born a mean fuck, you will probably always be one, and I guess that the Great Provider just made a Horlicks of the link-up between money and the 'what to do with it' gene. A bit like when he linked together the breathtaking football skills of George Best and the attraction of a bottle of beer, or the need for Elvis the Pelvis to consume fifty peanut butter baguettes laced with brightly coloured pills between 'Blue Suede Shoes' and 'Jailhouse Rock'. Fuck-ups happen, even in the holy production line.

Now I was lucky, in a way, because my money didn't come overnight. It started with a gradual easing of housekeeping restraints so that Tana could shop without working out the sums beforehand. She could impulse-buy and fill the kitchen shelves with things that were fun to buy, even if they never saw the light of day again. Norwegian wooden toothpicks, plastic swords for the olives, pink loo paper with the imprint of raspberries – that sort of thing.

Another aspect that was a contributing factor to Planet Spend was that, unlike a footballer who starts to fill the net every Saturday with pinpoint accuracy and suddenly finds that he is earning in a week was he was previously earning in a career, I was surrounded with people in everyday jobs. Moreover, I employed them, talked to them, listened to their dreams of becoming a sous-chef or a head waiter. Money wasn't their motivation. It was the need to better themselves. I was getting used to money in a three-dimensional world, and wasn't catapulted into the rarefied atmosphere of the film or rock star, where their earnings mean that they can employ someone to put toothpaste on their toothbrush.

I can guarantee that the first stop for the male achiever, when it comes to spending newly gotten wealth, is the car showroom. It's a convenient platform to embark on your show of wealth because you don't actually have to have the money in the bank. Chris has had a quiet, private-hire purchase man in the background, probably since before the First World War, who will always advance whatever it is that Chris needs, either for the company or for my cars. The money salesman is Roger Bradbury, a tall, balding, gentle man who only lends money to people whom he trusts. Chris has known him since 1976, and has never missed a payment, even during the three-day week – whatever that was – or the double-digit interest hikes of the 1980s and

1990s, or whatever other financial meltdowns Chris trots out when he gets morose. Roger has also become one of our best restaurant customers, though if he hadn't met us, he would probably have gone through life without ever eating out. I like to think that we've brought something to his life, just as he regularly brought shiny new Ferraris into my life.

Cars have always been my weakness. Women buy handbags, and rich people buy yachts. I buy cars, and dispose of them when I clear out the garage – sometimes with 300 miles on the clock and six months of repayments left on HP.

I have a really good friend called Tim, who works for a shiny car dealership. We get on well, and whenever there is a new model of Ferrari, he rings me up to give me first refusal. I can never say no. I used to get Chris to call Roger, but now I call him directly, as Chris gives me such earache, which is a laugh in itself. Being married to his daughter, I get the full low-down on how he bought cars when he was beginning to make money, how he went into Jack Barclay and bought a turquoise T2 for his thirtieth birthday, and then bought a green one six months later because he preferred the colour. On another occasion, he bought a yellow and black Panther de Ville and would drive it over to pick the kids up from school. They still don't really speak to him over that. In spite of what my friend Tim says, cars do cost you money. They are a fucking money drain.

My first real car was a Porsche 911, which I bought while I was still at *Aubergine*. Everyone knew that things were going well at the restaurant, but, of course, I was getting no real money out of it. Then, suddenly, along came a book publisher who not only volunteered to publish my first cookbook, but offered an advance. I used it to put down a deposit, and became the incredibly proud owner of a black Porsche. Everyone liked it, and I gave rides to anyone who wanted the buzz of 0–60 in five seconds along the King's Road. This went on for a few weeks, and then I began to realize the amount of petrol it consumed and the cost of parking this little monster in town. Added to that was the small matter of the standing order that depleted my bank account by a couple of thousand quid every month, without so much as a please or thank you. Not only that, but I had at least two and a half more years of this, and no one was excited by the car any more.

I sold it and lost about £10,000, and you would think that was a well-learned, expensive lesson. But it wasn't. I am such a silly arse sometimes. When I had the now famous Code 9 tax enquiry, which I referred to earlier on, Chris had to piece together the history of all the cars I had bought. It took him for ever, and I can imagine what the little tax man was thinking as he read through it. I bet he turned over the last page and thought, 'This guy needs therapy, but I'll nail the bastard for some more tax first.'

I also had a liking for watches, which is ironic, since I'm usually late for appointments. As with cars, they show you off a bit, but they don't cost so much to run. I also liked buying them for people who had helped me in a TV show or had a big birthday. I also remember getting carried away at a charity auction and buying a pink Asprey watch with a face circled with tiny diamonds. I probably paid about £35,000 for it, and it is so vulgar that I don't know what the fuck I shall ever do with it. Such are charity auctions. They are set up brilliantly to fleece those who can afford to give something in return for a five-minute warm feeling among a crowd of people who are wondering what the hell a chef is going to do with a pink, diamond-encrusted watch. And fuck me, he paid how much? Look out, Chris. It's your sixtieth soon.

I can't say that I spent a childhood flying in economy and always yearned for an upgrade because, of course, I never travelled anywhere, except to France, and that was on the Folkestone ferry. But I learned quickly, and after a few trips to Dubai, I understood that to turn right on a plane is completely in the wrong direction. The last time I did was on an Air India flight to New York. Frank Warren had invited Marcus Wareing and myself to come along to one of his fights at Madison Square Garden in New York at the last minute, and all I could get were these seats. Fuck me. They were at the back, by the loos, and that was probably the last time I ever went economy. Frank's boy won.

My airline romance grew with our association with Singapore Airlines. Whenever I flew over to Singapore for menu consultations, I found myself in one of the twelve first-class seats, and that was probably as good as it gets, as regards commercial flying. There was space for a football match, it had on-demand videos, and you didn't have to sit next to some fat person on his way back from the finals of a McDonald's stuff 'em down contest. But this cosiness comes at a price, and although my Singapore tickets were paid for by a grateful airline, other travels were not. As Chris and I explored further afield and began to travel more frequently at our own expense, the bills mounted. And they were worth every penny. This way of life included me, Tana and my mum, but not the kids. When we went on holiday *en famille*, they went economy or the half-stage between economy and business class. They have to experience that for a few years, and maybe they will become hungry enough to make money for themselves.

There have been exceptions to this family rule. As the Blackstone boys got richer, they began to acquire private jets. Ceriale didn't quite reach that league, but he was not above hiring them when the need arose. The first private jet I flew in was with him from New York to Florida. It made me think of when my sister Diane used to read me *Wind in the Willows* when I was a kid. Toad was always excited about some new mode of transport. The horse-drawn caravan, which Toad loved so much, was thrown on its side when the horse was scared shitless by the loud horn of a passing car. No one had ever seen a car before, far less ridden in one, and, immediately, Toad saw it as the way to travel. Well, that hasn't happened to me – the price tag for a private jet is just too fucking silly. But I am not above hiring one. Chris laughs his pants off when I try and justify the cost of taking Tana, the kids, Mum and Jimmy, and probably the nanny, in a private jet, because I always end up thinking that the most worthwhile part is driving down to Farnborough and straight onto the tarmac.

Chris and I very rarely fell out. We were too close for that, but in the early days, I sometimes got frustrated that, with all our apparent success, there never seemed to be any private money building up. Chris maintained that we needed to plough the money into the company, whereas I needed to see some tangible return with 'Gordon Ramsay' written on it. By stamping my feet loud enough and throwing the whole of Hamleys out of the pram, I had finally got a house that Tana and I owned. Now I wanted to buy other property, and, frankly, wasn't that just the thing to do in London, when all prices were going up weekly? So, we started to buy some property. Nothing much, but I did buy a beautiful pub called the Warrington Hotel, and I bought a big flat opposite *Royal Hospital Road*. I helped Mum buy a nice house, and I began to look at a little bit of property development. Chris always came in on these investments with me, and what he understood was cash flow. When I wanted to buy loads of pubs, he would hold back and say, 'Slowly, slowly, catch the monkey.' He knew the dangers of being stretched too tightly when there are so many projects taking place. Terminal 5 is costing one and a half big ones in investment, and, although we know it will be a success, what if …? The same for Versailles, Prague, Los Angeles and five or six other projects. The early days of *The Connaught* before we got ourselves sorted, still haunted me. The thought of it all going tits-up and being back to Square One would sometimes wake me in the middle of the night, and I would have a bad half-hour.

Did I ever waste money? Probably, but no more than most people lose some cash along the way. I don't think I could ever pile up huge flower bills or have fifty cars in the garage, but then, I'm not in that league. There are rich people, as in 'affluent', and there are rich people, as in 'diamond-studded teaspoons'. I know what I have in the bank, and I know what my outgoings are. If there is a healthy residue, then it stays there, and if there isn't, then I'll stop buying cars for a while.

There was, however, one occasion when I did something pretty stupid. Both Chris and I had a pal who had a pal who had a great idea. This was at the time when the electricity people first started selling gas and the gas people were selling electricity, and it was a free-for-all when it came to the cost. In fact, it seemed like anyone could buy and sell the stuff, as long as they could sign consumers up and prove that they had saved them money. We will save you 50 per cent of your current bills, and we then get 50 per cent of 50 per cent. So Pal of a Pal started a business that did nothing more than try and sell the cheapest tariff to the public. All he wanted to set it up was £40,000, and – I can hardly believe it – we saw this as one fucking good idea, and gave Pal of a Pal the money. Never heard from him again. Pal was upset, but just raised an eyebrow. After all, what was there to say?

When I was forty, I put on a big bash for family, friends and people who had been good to me. It was a great night, and, within reason, no expense was spared. The bill was high, and I remember thinking that, in its way, it was a celebration of how much my situation had changed in the past few years. Five years earlier I would have considered a spend like that reserved for the inhabitants of Hollywood or Bollywood, or for dreamers from Disneyland. But your perspective changes, and you find yourself considering something that would never have occurred to you, and, I have to say, it can be very pleasant. Life-changing? No, but I wouldn't necessarily want to go back.

What is enough money? I remember a chef coming into one of the kitchens about ten years ago. I couldn't stand the fucker, particularly when he told me that his wife had won £98,456 on bingo the previous night. He was in a total dream, working out all the things he would be able to do and how it would change his life. The truth was, of course, that his life would change very little. The money just wasn't enough, and he would realize that, sooner or later. Preferably before giving in his notice. How people cope when they win some proper money like £10 million on the lottery, I don't know, and it sounds dangerous to me. Changes like that, from having nothing to being very rich, need time for the recipient to get used to it all. No good finding yourself at the top of Everest in a flash, before you have a chance to put on your frost-free mittens and turn on your oxygen. Best to start at the bottom and gradually climb up. It's much more fun, too.

So, the answer is to increase your wealth and get used to it along the way. When you feel you have enough, and that day will come, enjoy spending it without any more stress. It's probably best not to get into the rut of earning money for the sake of it or using it as a barometer of how good you are at business. Business should be a means to an end, not a means to carry on with some pointless exercise because there doesn't seem to be a better way of spending your time.

CONCLUSION

WHEN I LOOK BACK on everything that has happened over the past ten years, there have been just a few too many mistakes for my liking, and if I had to sum up my business life to date, I would probably borrow that much-used phrase so loved by tired teachers, 'could do better'. For me, there is only one reason for looking back at the past, as far as business is concerned, and that is to make use of those experiences in making new decisions. Nostalgia is not a business term, and phrases like 'if only' have little relevance in the boardroom. The ultimate error is to disregard earlier actions because in there is guidance that you have paid for, sometimes at an eye-watering price.

If it is success you are after, it helps if you are a worker. I know there are people out there, highly successful people, who seem to have achieved great things with minimum effort, but I haven't a clue how they do that. I need to work hard, and I need to be seen to work hard by my staff. That way, everyone knows how high the bar is set. This in itself creates a bond with your staff, and without them, you have nothing. In a successful business, you need their respect and their loyalty. Achieve that, and you are well and truly on your way to success.

Working hard means nothing more than doing what you set out to do, but with an intensity of purpose that has been thought out beforehand. Working hard scrubbing pots to avoid front-line responsibilities will result in little more than a clean saucepan and is not what I am talking about. Your mind has to be in on the act, to understand the reason for working long, unsocial hours in an inhospitable environment, whether it is to learn, to gain experience or to become the very first among equals. It is not obsessive; it is a discipline that becomes part of your make-up and for which there is no alternative. I remember how I immediately understood the question 'Do you sincerely want to be rich?' Everybody wants to answer yes to the question, but they miss the point, which is the word 'sincerely'. They thought the question was simply, 'Do you want to be rich?' 'Sincerely' means that you are prepared to give everything to achieve riches, and this means working your fucking butt off. To put it another way, if you are to achieve a level of success that is above the norm, then you have to set disciplines that most people don't even want to hear about.

You have no money and no fame. All you have is this need to succeed, and it is burning a hole in your pants. While you work, keep your eyes peeled on the horizon for the next target. You need antennae that seek out the whisper of an opportunity, and it will come, believe me. A driven person is noticed like a noisy hornet on a summer's day, and someone will come up with a suggestion for the next part of your life. Just take care in assessing this someone, and don't be slow to ask all the questions.

I started *Aubergine* because, in those early days, it seemed to have everything that I wanted. It was the opportunity to do so much, yet what I achieved there nearly brought my downfall. I hadn't seen at first that, while I was enjoying a growing reputation, the owners were quietly enjoying the fruits of that reputation, just as I didn't appreciate, at that time, that around me I was grooming what was to become my greatest asset, a loyal and highly capable workforce. And there, like a teacher in front of a class, were my bosses, happily giving me free lessons in how to destroy a business. Be seen to do nothing other than schmooze around the dining room, take no interest in how the kitchen works and ignore the birthdays of your staff. This attitude soaked through me like vinegar, and the vanity that came with success in this tiny restaurant was beginning to suffocate me. That is exactly what happens when you grow too big for your suit: you need to find a bigger one.

One thing will always remain in my mind about the *Aubergine* story. This will sound as though my head is like a fat pumpkin filled with conceit, but I cannot help comparing the attitude of those Italian owners with Decca turning away the Beatles. Everyone knows the story because it was like shredding the winning lottery ticket, but here was a band of so-called businessmen kicking me in the goolies, rather than seeing what I had to offer. Proper treatment, paternal advice, financial equality and a generous contract could have ensured that I was retained for ever. And I was young and fucking daft enough to have signed myself away.

But I didn't, and that was partly luck. Never imagine for one moment that success doesn't need some luck. And never stop making your own luck, because luck follows those who are determined. Luck doesn't just happen, at least not the variety that I need. Luck is like a white truffle that needs sniffing out, and, once found, it has to be dug up and carefully cleaned. It will bring riches to the finder.

Thinking back to the Italians for a moment, there followed all sorts of recriminations that eventually came to nothing other than huge legal bills for both sides, but I remember, at one awards ceremony – I think it was the annual *Zagat Guide* launch – as *Royal Hospital Road* was named by Tim Zagat as the winner of 'Best Restaurant', Chris, that Machiavellian character, sidled up to one of the Italians and whispered, 'And you fucking lost him.' Probably ensured a limp dick for the rest of the guy's life.

The migration of the *Aubergine* staff, my staff, to *Royal Hospital Road* is worth further comment. I have already spoken about the bond that had grown between us because we had all suffered hardship together. The hardship was long hours, cold early mornings and few breaks in the working day. The money wasn't great, and we received little thanks from 'the owners'. We were all doing it together, and out of that grew a camaraderie that would live on for years. What else was it that persuaded each member of staff to step out into the unknown? I guess they didn't want to miss out on a continuation of the bonhomie, and there was a genuine feeling of excitement that we were breaking new ground. This excitement spread among the cooks, to the kitchen porters and through to the dining room staff. Everyone felt that this was their big chance, and no one wanted to miss out. A motivated workforce should be every employer's dream, yet it still remains the exception. Encouragement should be as important as the wages. People need money to live and motivation to build a life. There is one step further that must not be forgotten, and that concerns the recognition of your worth. If there is true devotion, then make sure the member of your team knows that you, the boss, have noticed. They don't need songs of praise all over the place, but you must spend some time with them or acknowledge that the team is incomplete without them. Being a piece of a jigsaw is one fucking great feeling.

The decision to move on is not the difficult bit. It is the direction you choose that can pose problems. Seeing through people can be as hard as looking through walls, and gut instincts are not always reliable. Have a look in someone's eyes and try to find out about their background, their motives, their history, and ask them direct questions. The replies might just tell you something, and your attitude certainly makes them realize that you are not afraid. I am no psychologist, but if you are not afraid, and if you are seen to be confident in yourself, pound to a penny, you will have the upper hand.

I was lucky in that my real break came with Chris. He was already successful, had a whole bunch of experience and was the father of Tana, my wife. To be honest, he also seemed to be just as excited as I was about what we were going to do, which was pretty fucking amazing, in that it was a totally new experience for him. Did I take a risk at this stage? Well, if I did, it certainly didn't seem like it, because Chris appeared outwardly confident in this foreign territory, and I was just busting a gut to get going.

When someone you trust holds out a helping hand, grab it. This is no time to be timid. When Pierre Koffmann offered me a deal, I felt he really wanted me to take it and succeed. Maybe someone had helped him once and he was remembering that. He had absolutely no reason to help me along, aside from selling his restaurant, and I got the distinct feeling that that was not his primary aim. If I had any doubts about that, why did he delay part of the sale proceeds, when everyone in business knows that the only safe payment in a deal is the payment that is received at the time of signature? Pierre took a flyer with me, and I shall always remember that. More importantly, I shall always try to be as giving to promising generations as they come my way. And had Pierre ever asked for a table for two for life in my restaurants, it would have been his with my compliments and eternal thanks.

The opening of *Royal Hospital Road* was not difficult for me. It was the distillation of everything that I had worked and trained for, and I was surrounded by talent. If we'd needed to recruit new staff in the dining room and train them, if we'd had to find a new brigade in the kitchen, it wouldn't have been so easy. This was a gentle introduction to business, and probably contributed to the confidence – the over-confidence – that led to the shambles of *Amaryllis* in Scotland. My earlier experiences in *Harvey's*, Paris and *Aubergine* were just the dress rehearsal for what was now unfolding, and I had learned my role well.

When the success that you have craved in opening your own restaurant begins to seep through, a strange thing happens. The feeling of success somehow disappears, and what seemed impossible now becomes attainable and almost ordinary. A similar experience comes with running. I look back to the days when Chris pulled me out of the kitchen in the early days of *Royal Hospital Road* and called me a fat bastard. Well, how charming was that? Not only that, but he started on one of his lectures about how any son-in-law of his was not going to be a fat slob, and, before, I knew it he had me running for my life every Sunday. In being so focused in the kitchen, tasting every dish that came to the pass, I had put on weight and hadn't noticed. Within weeks things were getting under control, and I knew this because I began to get competitive. I had been up in Chris's flat one day and little Christopher Hutcheson, one of Chris's grandchildren, had pulled out an old sock from his desk. The sock was stuffed with medals, bloody hundreds of them, from all the marathons Chris had run over the years. Suddenly I'm thinking that this old bastard is still running rings around me and that this can't carry on.

In time, I began to get close to him, but what I noticed was that, having run my first few marathons, what had seemed so impossible was suddenly no big deal, so I started looking further afield for longer distances. When Chris introduced me to the Comrades Marathon in South Africa, I viewed it as the most impossible run I could imagine. It was 56 miles straight off, well over a double marathon. But I went off and did it, and suddenly it didn't seem so impressive after all. It reminded me of one of the Marx Brothers, who said that any club that would take him as a member wasn't worth joining. So, having opened *Royal Hospital Road*, I suddenly realized it would never be enough for me. I had developed a taste for business and making money. Chris and I were now partners, of course, and I think that not only did he see how things were with me, but he was in absolute synch. He had always had his own business and was probably unemployable, in that he always wanted to be in control, but here we were together as a total match. We both brought different things to the table, so to speak, and it was these that made an extremely successful business partnership. I sometimes look back and realize that very few partnerships work in such close proximity. Ours did because there was mutual respect for each other's territory and field of expertise. Many people have said that we couldn't have done it without each other, and Chris always chimes in with the same old line, 'It would be much easier for Gordon to find another Chris than for Chris to find another Gordon.' He's wrong, simply because it is the togetherness that would be so difficult to replace. But I'm happy for him to carry on believing otherwise.

So, while we were awash with confidence, along came *Pétrus*. We hadn't been looking for it, but that faint scent of possibility revealed an extraordinary energy and passion to extend the empire from one restaurant to two. And that is what we did. I had Mark Askew attending to and maintaining the standards in the kitchen of *Royal Hospital Road*. He was as reliable as gravity, and it was he who allowed me space to grow the business, even at this early stage. If I wasn't getting involved in the launch of *Pétrus*, then I would be doing a photo-shoot for a new book or acting as a consultant to an airline or food supplier. This was a primary lesson for me: don't get so involved that you get sucked into a corner, emerging only once in a blue moon with a pasty face and still with only one restaurant. Years later, when we commissioned the Gordon Ramsay Holdings Cup for the person judged to have made the greatest contribution to the growth of Holdings, the first person to win it was Mark Askew. He had allowed me to do other things, confident that my first restaurant, my pride and joy, and one day to attain three Michelin stars, was in safe hands.

Glasgow was my first failure, and it taught me to never be afraid of admitting that things can and do go wrong. It's a simple chain that starts with the admission that this was a total tits-up situation, and this allows you to view what went on and come to some conclusions as to why it failed. This, in turn, helps you to ensure that such mistakes are avoided in the future. So, if you can't face the earlier, rather unpalatable fact that something went wrong, then you deny yourself the key to the classroom.

Analysing the pile of manure needs a notebook and a clothes peg. Stick the clothes peg on your nose and get on with it, because there will be a lot to learn from the mess. In apportioning the blame, there is only one place to start, and that is at the top. That's Chris and myself. By all means, look at the symptoms of the dying swan, but don't look anywhere else for the causes. The arrow came from us, and if words like vanity, conceit and lack of presence come to mind, then jot them down for future inclusion in the Gordon Ramsay bible, under the list of deadly sins. Lastly, if the post-mortem says that you failed to pull the plug before another £100,000 was flushed away, then score a spectacular minus ten points and hang your head in shame. Unsuccessful restaurants stand out a mile, and nothing but a total transformation will ever change this perception, as guests will smell failure and keep their distance. Anyway, we don't do half-full restaurants.

Making public relations work is a tricky manoeuvre. If I were to define what the term means to me, it would be the attempt to create a perception. There are times when it works magically, even if there isn't an ounce of truth in the press releases that are scattered in the streets, and there are times, perhaps most times, when the 'attempt', in my definition, fails to work. The best PR spreads good news about a favourite subject. Flick through *OK!* and *Hello!* magazines to see how true this can be. The worst PR is from the salvage squad, who have the task of converting public opinion from a perception of disgrace and ignominy to misunderstood perfection. That is just never going to happen.

Think twice before employing a PR agency. They are pricey, and guarantee nothing except a bill at the end of the month. They are forever thinking that the way to bring a restaurant before the public eye is to invite every C-list celebrity and journalist to multiple dinners at my expense, confident that the guests will go off and tell all their friends what a great place it is to visit. Of course it's great. It's free. It reminds me of when *Royal Hospital Road* had been open for a year or so, and a particularly insistent American journalist requested a table for two so that she could write us up in some American journal. I explained to the ever-patient Sauce Communications, our PR firm, that we were booked a month ahead, and I could not even think of complimentary dinners. It's just not what we do. The journalist persisted, promising that, if we didn't oblige, we'd miss out on a centre spread. I react well to this sort of sustained pressure, and I called the lady in question. With charm and patience, I booked her in for dinner on Saturday 11 May, and she was delighted. The only slight problem is that *Royal Hospital Road* doesn't open at weekends, and I think that somewhere we still have the letter that arrived the following week from Miss Centre Spread.

Having said that, if you have a great product or service, then go the PR route. Frankly, we couldn't operate without their contacts, and whenever there is a story to feed, they will know the best destination for it. Just don't confuse public relations and advertising. Remember that a good product might need a PR firm, but a weak product requires advertising.

As the lucky breaks get bigger, so do the risks. If your heart can live with the pace, then go for it, and remember the basics. *Gordon Ramsay at Claridge's* was a concept that, on the face of it, shouldn't have worked. It did work because we paid so much attention to all the little details that combine to bring success. The important point here, though, was that we could easily have sat back, content with the profits, and missed what real attention to detail could produce. The constant monitoring, the checking and course-correction led to an astonishing threefold increase in what was originally considered an acceptable profit. Our early reports from 'secret shoppers', guests who are planted to observe and write reports, were ridiculed, but we kept on, and gradually a picture emerged of the flawed areas of service. All it takes is the price of a table for two, and, in return, you have a comprehensive picture of how the public views you. It's like looking at your back in a mirror. It's a picture you don't often see, and it can be very revealing. Choose your shoppers carefully, as they need to be objective and calm. Also, prepare the way for their observations with a set of searching questions that have a direct bearing on the guests' dining experience. The secret shopper is used extensively throughout the group, and can cover a number of customer contact points, such as the reservation phone call. A call for a reservation is the first contact that a guest has with a Gordon Ramsay restaurant. How many rings does it take before the call is answered? Does the reservationist use the surname once it has been given, and does the call result in a booking? This type of information, linked to the statistics taken off the telephone system, will give full feedback to the reservations manager, who will always be looking for a perfect score: all phones answered within three rings and a 100 per cent call conversion to bookings. This might never happen, but it is what she will be aiming for.

In the early days, particularly after the opening of *Gordon Ramsay at Claridge's*, Chris's take on what happened in the restaurant, as opposed to the kitchen, was very useful. He did have this ability to understand what people looked for, rather than just great food and someone to pour the wine. I think it probably stemmed back to his days in printing, when he realized that what he sold, in terms of quality and price, was only part of what the customer was looking for. People need to like the people they deal with, and what better setting than a restaurant? It's incredibly easy for waiters to rise up through the ranks, from college to commis waiter and then up the greasy pole to restaurant manager, without ever realizing that they are one of the mainstays of the hospitality industry. That's the industry where the customer is always right. It is too easy to imagine that staff understand what their guests are looking for. A waiter is taught how to manage table settings, how to serve at the table, how to prepare bills and all the obvious disciplines associated with being a waiter. What is missing is an understanding of what it is like to be a guest – seated, ordering, watching the goings-on of staff, tasting each course, selecting wine and deciding whether to add a tip or not. An understanding will only develop if the waiter starts eating out, which is unlikely because it is expensive, or, of course, if he is trained and educated by his employer.

The employer should make it a priority that staff are not only confronted with the whole nine yards of consideration for his guests, but are taught how to deal with the questions that inevitably occur. How many times do you ask a waiter something slightly unusual and get back a confused reply? 'Is pollock the same as cod?' Blank face. 'Is Gordon in the kitchen?' Blind panic. These are moments that can be anticipated, and a cool response is needed to make the guest feel at home.

It has been a long time since our first long-distance transaction. Scotland came first and taught us two things. One was how to lose £750,000 in a hurry, and the other was to be careful when treading outside your known territory. Dubai, and later Tokyo, didn't depend on us for daily management. They demanded a line of Gordon Ramsay staff, guidance on the menus and occasional visits from me, but, apart from that, they ran themselves with their own codes and disciplines. But New York was different.

If I learned one thing, it was to do your homework thoroughly before jumping in. It is so easy to imagine that you will be able to muddle through, when, in fact, you need someone who can dismantle the whole operation and understand every nut and bolt. In New York, we simply didn't do this until well after the start-up, so there were constant surprises. Imagine racing a car and as it screams around the circuit, your pit crew are frantically reading the handbook to find out how to change the wheel. It's all too late, and that's what we tried to do in New York. Now before taking on foreign fields, we take ten different headings and detail every aspect until those who are charged with running the new territory know all that there is to know. That's one stage further than knowing all that they need to know. The ten different headings include employment law, property law, taxation, corporate structures, health and safety regulations, immigration, banking protocols, health insurance, liquor licensing and something else – but, to be honest, I've fallen asleep by then. That's why I employ the experts. It reminds me of Tana's sister, Olly, who was a pilot before starting a family. Tana tells me that when Olly was studying for her commercial pilot's licence, she had to learn how aircraft engines worked. It was a case of knowing everything that there was to know, rather than just enough for a pilot's needs.

I often speak about the importance of the word 'sorry' and how it is probably the most underused word in the service industry. Its considered use can win you more friends than any complimentary drinks, simply because people are not used to it. It's like holding a door open for a woman who may be so shocked at this rare show of manners in today's society that she scuttles through like a scalded cat. But there are limits to apologies, and once you have reached these limits, it's time for action, whoever the guest might be. A table of four guests at *Royal Hospital Road* came in at 1.30 p.m. for lunch. They chose the tasting menu, and worked their way through until around 4.30, when, just as the dessert was being served, they complained about a waiter who was ironing a tablecloth on one of the nearby tables in preparation for the evening service. The head waiter, Nicholas, went up, apologized and arranged for the ironing to stop immediately. Half an hour later, the party called for the bill and then disputed it, on account of the ironing incident. Nicholas pointed out that he had already deducted the coffees, the petits fours and the service charge, but didn't realize that he was taking on an Olympic-class negotiator. The bill-payer suggested a reduction of half of the £600 bill, and Nicholas declined. Eventually, the party got up to go, leaving their address but no payment. After several registered letters and eventually a writ issued for the unpaid bill, we all ended up in court. It was a painfully long process, and needed a further session before we were awarded the decision and the bill was paid. Why didn't I just take a commercial decision? Because we were right and they were out of order. Look at it in the context that, in nine years, it has only happened once, and it makes it easier to swallow. We got our £600, and it probably cost us £3,000 to obtain it. I just couldn't let it go. It wasn't personal, it was just what seemed right at the time.

Watching a small business like ours get bigger is like seeing a family grow. In time the household grows and needs a bigger house. If you run a business that has several branches, all of which need controlling, then centralize that control. It may seem expensive at first, but imagine how impossible it would be to bring uniformity to these outposts if each was to have an independent manager. I know of at least one prominent restaurant chain that only has a centralized accounts office. Everything else is arranged by the individual restaurant, and I haven't got a clue how they manage it. Chris was recently in the US, talking to the CEO of a very high-profile hotel chain. They had shown an interest in expanding their restaurant profile with our help, and declared that, of all the restaurant groups that they had examined, ours was the only one to have centralized all the administrative operations. It was something that we seemed to slip into after we started up *Gordon Ramsay at Claridge's*, and recognized immediately that, for us, it was the way to go. The only difficulty is to get the timing right. You really need to have a clear idea of where you are going, and that is far from easy. When *The Connaught* came along, it was a surprise, but we managed to fit its administration into our existing framework. When we were subsequently hit with *Boxwood*, *The Savoy Grill* and the moving of *Pétrus* to The Berkeley, we needed luck, and that came along as though it were stage-managed. Our offices at Catherine Place in Victoria had six floors, three of which we occupied. The other three were full of accountants who had moved in and, on the stroke of twelve, realized that it was the wrong place for them. They decamped, and suddenly we had the whole building.

So, the centralized office control not only worked but was viewed as an extremely sane way to organize ourselves. The other, perhaps unusual, initiative was to give our key players a share of the action. This meant that Marcus Wareing, Angela Hartnett, Stuart Gillies and Jason Atherton received shares in the businesses that they were heading. Not, you might say, an original plan altogether, but, strangely, something that you don't come across very often in the restaurant business. What it meant for the chefs was they had become true chef patrons, and were guaranteed that, during the life of their restaurant, they would have a share of the net worth. They never had to invest, other than their initial purchase of shares, and, in time, their shareholding would be more valuable than any pension that we could have arranged. What it meant for the group was that we had the loyalty of the most amazing chefs, whose careers would span many years. It is a policy that we shall continue for as long as we can attract chefs of that calibre.

We made a mistake with one chef. He was a specialist in a field of cuisine that we were not acquainted with, other than through visiting his restaurant. He came off the hinges with his then employer and came under our wing. He didn't know how we did things, and in a very short period of time after we had set him up in his own restaurant, it became clear that we had made a very big mistake. I don't mean that he couldn't cook. He was a fantastic cook, but the disciplines were missing. Our mistake was to bring in an outsider whose idea of kitchen order was very different from ours. It cost a great deal of money, as mistakes in restaurants tend to do, before we cut him loose and licked our wounds. The upside of this was an intense reminder of what we had in our team, who, over the years, have learned the significance of two words: 'shout' and 'love'. You can't have one without the other for any length of time, and they understood that.

What *The Connaught* taught me was never to be frightened by size. It wasn't that we were looking at a huge hotel. Far from it – it only has ninety-two rooms. But we were looking at our first venture outside the confines of a restaurant. We had to consider all the food and beverage requirements of a hotel and its guests, twenty-four hours of the day. There was nothing there that we couldn't do, but we knew it wouldn't be easy to adopt the confidence that comes with experience and that propels staff through the dining room without a period of settling in. Fortunately, what with the on-site builders and all the kerfuffle, there was a degree of latitude that we needed. Within weeks we were there, although it took considerably longer before we made money.

New York was like *The Connaught* in many ways. A whole food and beverage operation, but on a larger, much larger, scale. The only real differences were that, in New York, we were in for big bucks, and we had to handle the union situation, but it became a measure of how size should not frighten us off.

Chris has a favourite story of how he started in business and how his first real lesson was learned. He had moved to Mayfair, where his mum worked, in 1954. He was pretty free to come and go as he pleased in a London very different from today, and at the age of seven, he started a business running errands for the local tarts. While they waited on the streets, Chris would pop around to the local Curzon cinema for their cigarettes so that they wouldn't lose their place when the punters were about. This, Chris confirms, was a healthy little business until 1959, when the girls disappeared overnight and Chris was walking about wondering what the fuck had happened. Too young to read the papers, he was not aware of the introduction of the Street Offences Act, which banned prostitutes from the streets so, in one minute, he had lost the only business he had.

The lesson, of course, was never to have only one string to your bow, and the relevance, from my point of view, was developing my intellectual property portfolio, in addition to my core business. As with all successful 'other interests', the IP activities linked closely to the restaurants, and all came under the Gordon Ramsay brand. What is necessary (and certainly not so easy) is to create a brand with what you do and how you do it, because that could become the most valuable asset you own. Just look at the times a well-known brand has gone tits-up and the business goes into receivership. What is the first thing that the scavengers look for as they pick through the bones of a commercial wreck? Inevitably, it's the name or the brand that someone will buy.

Having established or bought the brand, the trick is then to ensure that the crucial elements associated with it remain strong in the public's perception. Buying the Rolls-Royce brand and then appending it to the equivalent of a Ford Mondeo is going to fool no one. When I decided to extend our restaurant operation to include more informal styles of cuisine, the most important protection was to show that our high standards of service and value were still there. The combining of great flavours into interesting dishes at reasonable prices had become our hallmark, and that was not to change. There was no dilution, just a different market, but with the same brand.

We are all liable for tax, and it has always amazed me that, in the area of trade, of buying and selling, everyone looks to see what the profit is, but never seems to take into consideration the tax. It just puts such a different slant on things. If I am asked to go to Poland to make a speech and the fee is £50,000 and I am not sure if I want to go, I do my sums. This would go like this: £50,000 less 15 per cent for my agent, less 40 per cent tax, leaves me with £25,500. So the figure I really have to consider is marginally over 50 per cent of the fee offered. No rocket science here. But while we are on the subject of tax, your close attention should extend to the whole boring but vital subject of numbers. They are your way of measuring success, and unless you ensure a proper accounting system, you are depriving yourself of the biggest tool in the chest. We have brought into our monthly figures the science of indicators, numbers that everyone can follow and understand, together with the signs that they send out. Food margins are just the ratio of the cost of the raw ingredients, compared to the food sales generated by the restaurant. These figures vary from location to location, season to season, and good month to bad month. Make sure that, whatever business you are in, the people responsible for putting everything together also get to see the indicators. Staff costs are another item, and when treated as an indicator, with a norm for the ratio of staff salaries against turnover, any overstaffing can be quickly identified and challenged.

Added to that, make sure that there is someone around who knows about money. It is amazing how banks will rip you off because you need £50,000 transferred to France. Is it cheaper to arrange the conversion to euros first? Can you send it by BACS, or how much does it cost to send it by CHAPS on the same day? You have £350,000 in your current account for a week? Have you heard of overnight deposits, or do you want to make a present to the bank? Just housekeeping, really, but who wants all that hassle unless you know what you are doing? And, as you get bigger, you will need a finance director, an expensive addition, but if you have the right one, he will bring you a handsome return on your investment.

I have a PA. She looks after my diary, my expenses, my flights here and there, and makes sure I know the names of the people I am going to meet. She's a darling, and neither Tana nor I could manage the day without her. I have another shadow called Mark Sargeant, who came to me in the *Aubergine* days. His real job is chef de cuisine at *Gordon Ramsay at Claridge's,* where he has been the driving force behind this successful restaurant since its opening. He is like a gypsy's whippet, thin as a thread and so packed with electricity that he cannot keep still for a moment. He is one of those rare chefs who has had a full education, and can do things like reading, writing and arithmetic. In the early days, he would sometimes help me with the conversion of commercial recipes into the domestic version, ready for my home economist to test before sending off to the publisher. He still does this, and also helps me prepare columns for the Saturday *Times*. The guy is my lieutenant, and is always there to help me prepare for cookery demonstrations or private dinners. He understands me, and can react without me having to mention a thing when the occasion arises. He can represent me because he is funny and not too grown up, and he is there to prove the point that everyone needs back-up and support.

War Games

On the far side of Chris's office, there is a large glass desk. On it are stacks of papers, some piled high and others consisting of no more than a few sheets. These represent future plans, which will unfold over the coming months or end up in the bin, shredded and forgotten. The piles are updated daily, and as draft contracts arrive, they are stacked, ready for the next mark-up, along with numbers sent up from the projections desk on the accounts floor. Occasionally a pile is removed and placed in a red box to signify that the deal has been signed, the project is beginning to unfold and we have another player in the group. On top of each pile is the checklist showing the state of play in each case. The theory is that nothing advances to 'Go' without a completed checklist, but sometimes that doesn't quite happen. The bright side is that a year ago there was no checklist, just a collection of papers and a general feeling that most things were probably in place. We are travelling through space at the speed of light nowadays. All these arrangements are the result of spilt blood. We learn, but usually the hard way, and perhaps that is the best way forward. A bit like an unruly child, as someone once said to me, or probably about me.

This is my favourite part of the office, and it is where Chris and I play war games. I can walk in at any time and be updated on where we are with any particular deal, and

I can get excited about what I see or decide to pull the plug. At present, there are nine projects, which, if they all come off, would add a further £50 million to our turnover. There are two separate piles on the left side of the glass desk, and if they come off in all their glory, they will dwarf the other nine by adding £100 million to the group's turnover.

The T5 pile is, by far, the highest. The build for *Gordon Ramsay's Plane Food* at T5, the abbreviation for Heathrow's Terminal 5, has now begun. We have issued the first cheque for £500,000 to the construction company, and the huge concrete bay on the sixth floor of this vast new terminal is filling with materials and men dressed in steel-toecapped boots, Day-Glo yellow jackets, white gloves, protective glasses and hard hats. I have been there already, and I can hardly believe the size of the place. It is just fucking breathtaking. The luggage carousels have been installed for at least a year, and are now running with suitcases all day long to make sure that this vital facility, the one that airports so often get wrong, will work successfully from Day One, 27 March 2008. The ticket machines are all there, and have been mothballed, ready for next year. The T5 pile on the glass desk is about to move on into its red boxes, but, before that happens, we squint over the drawings once more and try and visualize how this will all end up looking. The investment is over £2 million, and we shall need to fill this air-side restaurant from the 85,000 passengers who will walk through the terminal each day. The challenges have been discussed over and over again. How to feed passengers in forty-five minutes, tops, from a Gordon Ramsay menu at a reasonable price and without the use of gas is the current issue. There is no gas in T5, and I don't imagine it's because they forgot it. The security clearing of staff, the supply of daily deliveries and the training of staff to deal with ten different currencies were last month's concerns.

Next to the T5 pile is the *Devonshire* pile, representing our latest pub acquisition. Well, I say that, but no deal has yet been signed. At present, during due diligence, we have found that there is more building to do than we had imagined. The pub, perhaps understandably, is not in such great shape, and a higher budget might mean that we have to go back to renegotiate the price. In the meantime, the lawyers keep at it, challenging each other's lack of full stops and, as we have said before, spending time in a dark room thinking about sex. There are also concerns regarding its potential trading. As with *The Narrow*, its historical trade has gone downwards of late, which is why it's on the market, and our mission is to turn things around. It is situated within a short walk of Chiswick High Street, and we feel confident that we can revive its lunchtime fortunes, after which we'll turn our attention to the evenings. And after that, we'll look at breakfast as an option.

Los Angeles, City of Angels and excruciatingly slow attorneys, has been part of our war games for nearly a year. The new venture will be the sister hotel to the New York London Hotel, but only in name. Everything else will be very different and in line with a sunny climate and the

Sunset Boulevard culture. The biggest tick will be against the 'no unions' box, and I look forward to meetings about our American adventures that don't start with 'Union Concerns'. Fine dining doesn't sit comfortably in LA. We are learning about sushi and light, healthy foods for skinny people. We are learning about interesting, non-alcoholic drinks and, most importantly of all, banqueting and function management and Oscar parties. Everything over there on the West Coast seems easier than New York. The pace is more leisurely, and we must adapt to the city that has brought me such success on the television screen. However laid back it may seem, though, there are some class acts about, and nothing better to showcase that then Wolfgang Puck's *Spago*, which provides great clues to the direction we are heading with the forty-five-minute menu for T5. It has taken us a fucking long time to get this far, but by the end of 2007, we should be ready with a checklist full of ticks, an opening date, and I am sure Catherine Zeta-Jones will be stopping by to shoot the breeze. I dream on.

If you want to talk opposites, just move on to the next pile, and there we have Prague, where I am due to open in November. What was known as *The Renaissance* has now closed down, while the builders rip out its heart and transplant a whole new concept. It's a Blackstone purchase, and with its sudden swoop on the Hilton Group, with its 2,700 additional hotels, for $20 billion, it may yet become branded as a Conrad, a Waldorf or just a plain Hilton. One way or another, they are bigger than us and make my little pools of excitement look like small beer, but who knows what is around the corner?

The Versailles project involves taking over the whole food and beverage operation of the Trianon Palace, just 15 kilometres outside Paris. In many ways, the labour issues reflect those in New York, with all sorts of spikey HR problems that, frankly, I leave in their entirety to the lawyers. It is going to be difficult enough to produce a menu that will withstand the French press, who will be anxious to ridicule *les Rosbifs*, and I look forward to taking them on in *Waterloo II, the Sequel*. The Trianon Palace is beautiful and is undergoing middle-age cosmetic surgery. I have yet to visit it, which highlights an extraordinary problem in that I rarely get to see any possible project ahead of Chris. He can breeze into any place like he's the insurance man, and no one knows him. If I turn up, everyone immediately thinks I am about to move in. Chris, the little fucker, loves this, and offers to draw me pictures. What he also says is that, when a new project is planned, he never likes to tell me until things are certain to happen. He knows that, in my excitement, I find it fucking difficult to keep it to myself. I want the world to know. He tells me that this is not good with regard to the negotiations and the staff situation. OK. I've got it.

The smallest pile is for Amsterdam. There is this fabulous little hotel called The Pulitzer tucked away beside one of the canals, and it will be there that we establish our first base in Holland later in 2008. This has been put on the back burner because there are planning complications and there is already so much on our plate that the delay is welcome news. And why do we want to do something there? Well, it just so happens that Holland is my biggest market for cookery books outside the UK. I have no idea why, but the Dutch just love them, so perhaps this move makes sense.

The brighter hotel operators in the world, after years of running their own restaurants, have worked out that the best option for any aspiring hotel is to bring in a restaurateur, and preferably a well-known chef, to run that part of the operation. This, clearly, has been a philosophy that has brought great benefit to us, and I must have said a million times that we do restaurant reservations and leave the problems of hotel occupancy to the hotelier. That, after all, is what they do. The only problem is that I have suddenly found a hotel – a very, very small hotel – and I want to take it over. Of course, attached to it are two restaurants, a retail outlet, private dining areas and a huge bar, but nevertheless, we are crossing a line that we have previously avoided. If we go ahead, the checklist will extend to new areas of expertise and the strain on my head office will increase. But it is an opportunity and, as I have described earlier, isn't that what business growth is about? In the meantime, I shall find the staff who could bring our disciplines and standards to this new area of operation and see where we are a year down the line.

Just along from *Royal Hospital Road* is a small, discreet bistro called *Foxtrot Oscar*. It had been there since the early eighties, largely as a club for minor royals, socialites (are these now referred to as celebrities?) and some members of what used to be Fleet Street's finest. It was a bottle of wine, steak and kidney pie, chips and a lazy afternoon type of place under the ownership of Michael, an old Etonian but nevertheless delightful 'mine host', who had seen that those days were over and called me for a chat. It was a place that, in the early days of *Royal Hospital Road*, I would escape to for a coffee and catch-up with the late Nigel Dempster, whose sharp pen was always poised to put me in my place. Michael now wanted me to buy *Foxtrot Oscar*, which seemed a great idea if nostalgia was to be the currency. But I had a better idea. What we needed to do was put together a concept bistro with what I have always thought to be a fabulous name and find a hotel chain that might be looking for such a brand. *Foxtrot Oscar* in Royal Hospital Road would be fitted out as a working showroom because, even with the best will in the world, the single restaurant was never going to make me a rich man. So the pile on the desk is growing daily, and the checklist for *Foxtrot Oscar* is nearing completion.

Finally, there is one pile left – not very high, but neater than any of its neighbours. On top is a blank piece of paper to shield its contents, so confidential is this small stack. A new project arrived at the beginning of the week, and it has the purple fast-track box nearby, as it is in need of our immediate attention. There are just two weeks before the subject of this proposal is plunged into receivership, with the break-up of all the assets and, more tragically, the business, with all its staff, suppliers and customers. For my team, everything is sidetracked while they crunch the available numbers, look at the liabilities, both on the balance sheet and the ones hidden away in some black hole, as always happens in these situations, and, of course, talk to our bankers. There is a large asset value, and somewhere we haven't been told the full story. The story will unfold, and in the next few days we shall make a decision whether to go for this or not.

How fucking exciting is that for a chef?

One Year Later

I have just reread 'War Games', which took up the last pages of the hardback edition of *Playing with Fire*, and it is about things that seem a thousand years ago. As I write, Terminal 5 has just opened. A huge metropolis in itself, with Prada, the usual suspects from Bond Street and Rodeo Drive, Harrods, in dazzling diamond white, and £2 million of what I would have referred to as 'dosh spent', but now refer to in more dignified terms as an 'investment', on my T5 restaurant, *Gordon Ramsay's Plane Food*.

But, two weeks earlier, before the apocalyptic chaos brewed by BA and BAA in their bright, shiny new depository for long-suffering customers and their disappearing luggage, we had, in a way, taken on a bigger challenge. We had opened up in France. Actually, in Paris. Well, in Versailles, which is but a 15-kilometre cab ride from the centre of Paris.

I am used to the critics arriving on the scene, trying to make a name for their strangulated egos by showing that they caught the first bus to a new restaurant. Nowadays, I am also used to reading their accounts of an experience that is more a chicane around the fact that they are failed chefs, lifelong members of 'my name doesn't matter, but I am an alcoholic', or the very occasional food writer who hasn't got a personal agenda or chip on a hunchbacked shoulder and just writes about what is on the menu. But *mon Dieu*! A few days before Versailles even opens, I read that some French hack who finds it difficult to understand the difference between *pain au chocolat* and *poo de chien* has decided to take the restaurant that hasn't yet opened to pieces. Fortunately, as the restaurant opens, the *Daily Telegraph* sends Jasper Gerard in, and he tells his readers that all is well.

But back to T5. The Queen has been along, and so have several Important People to anoint the extraordinary building. We have already won the unofficial award for the very best loos in Heathrow, though I suspect, in reality, they are the best in the whole of West London. The restaurant is so different to anything that we have done before in almost every respect. Few airline passengers arrive with starter, main course and dessert in mind, so we have a forty-five-minute slot in their itineraries to feed and impress them before they go on their merry ways. What do people like to eat before going to Europe on a two-hour flight, or to LA on a thirteen-hour long haul? Such questions have occupied the minds of our chefs and the operations team for the past three years. What should we put on the floor to withstand half a million feet, followed by their wheely luggage? How do we protect the tables from laptops, from upturned purses dispensing foreign shrapnel, and the chairs from squirming bottoms of a quarter of a million guests as they hear that their planes have been delayed by an hour?

We have been open for nearly five hours on the opening day of T5 before the first restaurant journalist rolls in on pole position for the first opinion. They probably arranged a day trip to the Channel Isles, just to be ahead of the pack, to write a review not worth the space it was written on some godforsaken blog. I hope the hack enjoyed Jersey or, even better, took a long haul to Wangawanga, never to be seen again.

The Devonshire is one of our pubs, a small, pretty building tucked away behind Chiswick High Street. As with much of what we are doing at present, it is experimental. We want to see what the effect is of a pub serving good food without being located on the main drag. Will people go a bit further down the road, or have we opened a white elephant? The answer appears to be that good food will win through. There is nothing trendy or flashy here. Just good value for those working or living in the surrounding area. It signals well for future plans to expand our operation to include small, select pubs like this, which might otherwise never have been used, since pubs can no longer offer a refuge for smokers.

This year's big opening for us in the States will be on Sunset Boulevard, Los Angeles. We have been working on it for two years, and we are almost there. It is situated in what used to be the Bel Age, a big pink hotel that badly needed the full monty of cosmetic surgery. It had a strange history, probably best summed up by the fact that the seventh floor had never been used. It was just one huge empty shell with no walls. Apparently, the original developers never got planning permission for this particular floor, although there are floors fully in use above. Only in America.

The hotel was bought as part of the Wyndham Group by our friends Blackstone, and will soon be opened as *The London* (*West Hollywood*). We will handle the complete food and beverage operation, including the restaurant, as we are already doing in New York. However, there is one very big difference: there are no unions, which just makes life less complicated – a bit like telling a patient that they can have anaesthetic before their operation.

With all the filming that I have been doing in LA, and with the opening of *The London*, I decide to look at buying a house out there. In my mind, it would be part investment and part just somewhere to stay. With the ever-weakening dollar, it hurts to take US earnings back to the UK, where their worth is cut in half. So I find myself a realtor and, with

Tana, start the search for a house. I am just beginning to hear the new term 'credit crunch', and soon I see that it is hurting Americans even at the top end of the property market. We find a place in Bel Air and set about the process of a house purchase. Over to Chris, who then spends many hours going through what seems like never-ending procedures. He even goes over to take a look at the property, and is tickled by the fact that it has a security system with CCTV that will screen pictures via the web to anywhere in the world, just so that you can make sure that the gardener has mowed the lawn. It's a brand-new property, but it is still necessary to bring in a battalion of surveyors to check out every aspect, from the chimney-stacks to the roof tiles. Each separate surveyor requires up-front payment, and then there are about five million words to read and a picture-book of every feature, from a plug socket to the self-cleaning lavatory. Chris asked what it was that got self-cleaned. Apparently, no one thought that he was funny. No change there, then.

And so it went on. We started to list the running costs, from housekeeper to pool-cleaner, and then came the straw that broke what was becoming too heavy a load for the poor fucking camel. The 'tremor insurance' was $78,000 a year. That's on top of the normal, everyday insurance, and so we decided there and then to call a halt to proceedings. There were other problems with blocked drains and the small matter of the growing credit crunch. Would this mean that our 'investment' slid downwards in a southern spiral as soon as we had purchased the pile? Chris had the job of calling our realtor friend to tell him the sad news.

But the credit crunch didn't stop there. At home, we were expanding rapidly. The problem with that happening is that it can attack your financial soul in two ways. The renovation of old kitchens in old hotels can unleash an unending catalogue of horrors. Fuck me. If I have heard the wail of 'over budget' once, I have heard it every day for the past year. The problem is that, once you start a project, there is rarely any easy way back. The sudden discovery of asbestos is about as damaging as finding that the kitchen is built on some protected Roman remains, and everything comes to a halt while the builders work out how much they can tuck you up. This is a relentless part of what we do, and suddenly we were struggling. A call to our bank seemed to release panic instead of more money and, before we knew it, what was no more than a request for a bit more flexibility brought in an avalanche of SWAT teams and men in suits to pore over the figures.

Their corporate department came up with the brilliant idea that we part with some of our equity to bring in further funds. That is, while we sweat away with labour pains during the delivery of our new *enfants*, we sell a lump of equity to some gold prospector for a fraction of the share value that will be realized two years down the road. Well, it would have been good for the bank, no doubt, but that was not what we were about, and they could go fuck themselves with that particular piece of Einstein banking theory.

It was time to move on to global bankers, and so that is exactly what we did. There were people out there who, it seemed, could see the bigger picture, and by the time they had run their eyes over everything, I began to realize that we really did have a strong, vibrant group that was attractive to big banking groups – at least those who weren't paralysed in the headlights of the demon credit-cruncher. Definitely a lesson there: don't assume that all bankers are big and bulletproof. They can make mistakes as easily and, unfortunately for the investors, the financial papers are full of such stories in the US and the UK.

The Narrow is a pub towards the Canary Wharf end of London. It sits right on the Thames as it swirls along in a big S-bend towards what used to be the Millennium Dome. Now, good pub sites – and this was the very first one that we looked at – are not always easy to spot. We first saw the availability of *The Narrow* on the Internet. No pushy estate agent there. Just a rather forlorn building, tucked behind towers of new apartments and with very little footfall passing. But it did have some interesting features, including a huge stone terrace and one of the best river views anywhere. It also had a reverse premium to entice some bidder to go for this site, and we jumped.

We gave it tender loving care. We made it comfortable, put in a shiny new kitchen, decorated it inside and out, and put in an upstairs dining room. To these cosmetic touches we added a great menu and some diligent, well-trained staff in the kitchen and at front of house. And hey fucking presto. From Day One we were inundated. Five-thick at the bar, all baying for a drink. The restaurant critics did their best to give us a hard time, but it was difficult for them, as everyone was voting with their knives and forks.

The takings during the warm evenings were phenomenal, and we were suddenly faced with the reality that while the weather was good we would make money, but what would happen when it was too cold to sit out on the terrace? In addition, we had become victims of our own success, and the dining room was just too small. We were having to refuse some of the 350 daily calls for a reservation, and people were just getting pissed about having to book for just a pub. So we thought a little out of the box and applied for planning permission for a large conservatory to cover half of the terrace. We got the permission, dug deep and spent £200,000 on expanding with a warm winter view and another sixty covers. *The Narrow* soared into the stratosphere, and we had removed the seasonality in one swift move. And then Chris explained to me that somehow we had missed it in the lease, but next door to the pub was a large covered car park capable of taking twenty-five cars. It belonged to *The Narrow* and it was all ours. The story just got even better.

Our opening in Prague was with some trepidation. The first viewing of the hotel had been with some disbelief: could such a dump be turned into a half-decent destination for one of our restaurants? But Chris, as ever, had faith in the restorative powers of a Blackstone makeover, and as sure as gun's iron, the ugly duckling appeared looking like a stunning catwalk model, strutting her stuff right through the middle of this beautiful, historic town. As is the case with most of our new sites nowadays, we took over the complete food and beverage operation, and, on the first floor, we had banqueting and private dining facilities sufficient to host the United Nations, the Olympic Committee, the Vatican and most of the Rangers fans, all in one sitting. We moved the *maze* concept in there, with Phil Carmichael, who had been Jason Atherton's Number Three in London. It was his big chance, and he seized it around the neck with a passion to succeed that could only mean one thing, and that was success.

Foxtrot Oscar is a small site sitting but a few doors along from my restaurant on Royal Hospital Road. Its author was Michael Proudlock, an old Etonian who, in spite of that drawback, had a bucketful of charm to help him through life. The old *Foxtrot Oscar* had run its course. Michael hadn't the cash to revamp it, and called me up to see if I was interested.

There was only one thing that interested me in the rundown hole in the wall, and that was the name. Fuck me, *Foxtrot*. We were meant for each other. So it entered into Gordon Ramsay's House of Experiments to see if we could somehow turn this into a merry concept that could expand beyond the confines of Chelsea.

What we looked at doing was to come up with a flatpack concept that could be put together easily and which would allow for the important factors of staff training, an attractive venue and a simple, good-quality, well-cooked menu. And this is what we launched as first base.

Holy hell. Within the first few days, we were visited by a whole canteen of restaurant critics, and I use the word 'critics' in the full sense. They just didn't get it, which was hardly surprising, as I hadn't written 'experimental' all over the walls. They judged it as a makeover of the old club, and said that I should be ashamed of myself. Looking at the early design, it was a bit spartan and bright, but what is experimentation all about? The fabled Ceriale from Blackstone took one look and was heard to say, 'Fucking lucky he can cook.'

So it's back to the drawing board, as far as the design is concerned, but *Foxtrot Oscar* is still open and doing rather well. Why? Because the core product is good and will remain so.

In the middle of all these new projects, we suddenly got a phone call from some English guy in France, telling us that there was a three-Michelin-star chef who was looking to sell up. He wanted to know if we would be interested in looking at buying his whole shooting match, including a couple of hotels, a golf course, a jam factory, vineyards and a centre of gastronomic excellence. Chris was off like Jack Shit on the next Eurostar with some of the team to explore this alluring situation. They met the chef, toured the two sites, buggied around the golf course and came back to London to crunch the numbers. It advanced past 'Go', and

I went down myself. It was an interesting set-up, but full of what were, for us, sizeable holes – a lesson on what not to do. This poor chap, after years of running an incredibly successful restaurant in a small hotel, had been tempted to expand with a partner to buy another hotel, which was miles from his centre of operations, and to operate it together with an 18-hole golf course, clubhouse and, no doubt, many other distractions. It had gone tits-up, and we could see no way of putting it back on the rails without spending an amount that would be beyond recovering. Once money gets short, all sorts of problems occur and compound until you are left with a whole load of papered cracks all ready for little kids to stick their fingers through.

Interestingly enough, when I went down there, I was riding around the 18-hole course on a golf cart with Nick Fletcher, our new finance director. It was a beautiful day, and the course looked stunning. I mentioned, just in passing, that this all looked good, and why weren't there any people playing this game that I knew nothing about? Nick just looked at me and said that it was a crap course. It was full of soaking bogs and everything that proper golfers don't want. So that was it. I was looking to buy something that I knew sod all about. *Au revoir*.

But something I did know about, which became probably the most exciting project of the year, came in the purchase of Tante Marie, a traditional cookery school down in the wilds of Woking, in Surrey. Here was a golden opportunity to attract large numbers of new recruits to the hospitality industry, from Letitia, who wants to become a good wife, to Jeremy, who has decided to blow his redundancy money from his hedge fund flop to change career and become a chef. Not only would we offer great courses, but we would also guide them into a fast-track career with Gordon Ramsay Holdings – all our recruitment problems solved at a stroke. Maybe not quite that easy, but definitely an opportunity that made me think that, within three years, we could have a whole fucking university.

Index